CHRISTMAS A-Z
Bible Crafts, Games and Puzzles

by

Dee Leone

illustrated by

Veronica Terrill

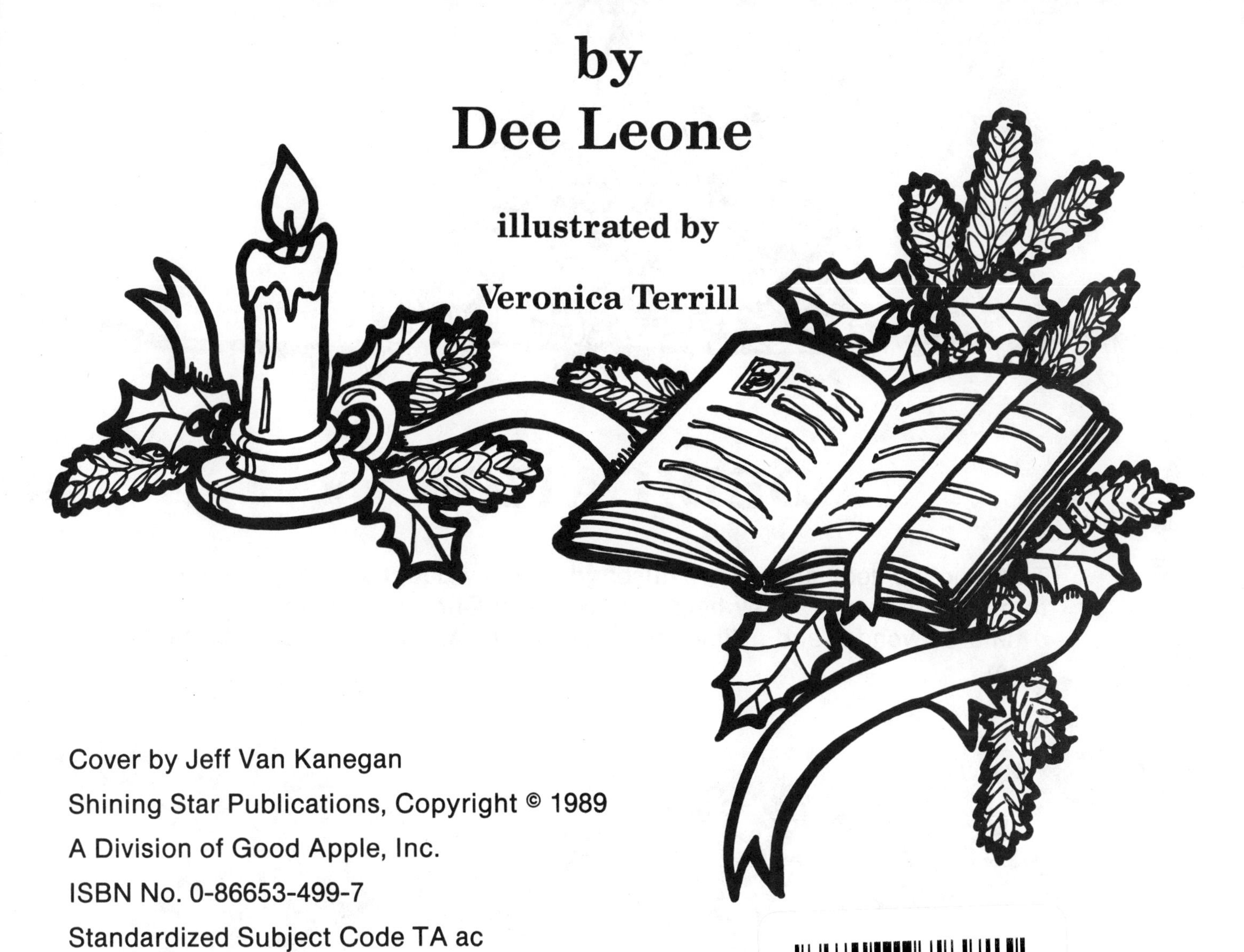

Cover by Jeff Van Kanegan

A Division of Good Apple, Inc.

ISBN No. 0-86653-499-7

Standardized Subject Code TA ac

Printing No. 987654321

Shining Star Publications
A Division of Good Apple, Inc.
Box 299
Carthage, IL 62321-0299

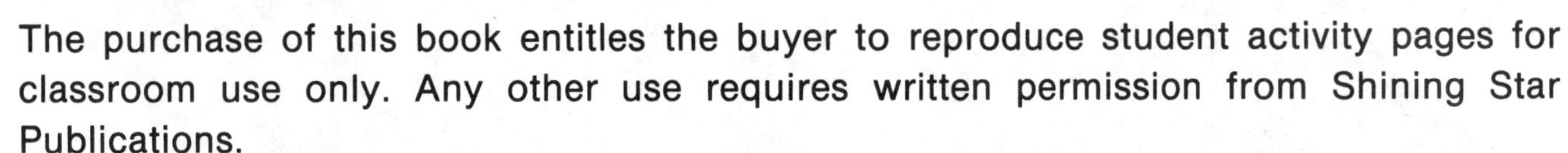

Unless otherwise indicated, the King James Version of the Bible was used in preparing the activities in this book.

DEDICATION

This book is dedicated to my husband Joe, my daughter Rachelle and to my whole family. They help to make each Christmas a time of love, a time of wonder and a time for treasured memories. May God bless them.

TABLE OF CONTENTS

TEACHING TIPS

This book contains a variety of ideas and activities which can be adapted to serve the many needs of teachers and students involved in Christian education. A few suggestions for the use of each section are given on this page and the following page.

The poem can be used to educate children about the Nativity story. It can be used as a choral reading or incorporated into a Christmas program. Each child can illustrate a different verse or do the suggested craft activity. Then, each child can read his or her verse and present the completed project to parents or younger students. A slide of each finished project can be made and used as part of a special assembly or celebration. The poem can also be integrated into other areas of the curriculum. In the area of language arts, for example, the verses can be used in the identification of rhyme, proper and common nouns, etc. Since each verse of the poem emphasizes a different letter, the verses are perfect for handwriting or calligraphy practice. They can also be a good source for spelling words. Sections of the display can also be used on bulletin boards or student-made greeting cards.

The art circles can be simply colored, or suggested craft ideas can be used. The patterns can be miniaturized and used as stickers. (Stickers can be made by applying a mixture containing equal amounts of water and glue or mucilage to the back of each sticker). The miniaturized circles can also be used to decorate lids to form ornaments. Small versions can be used for bulletin board borders or hung as Christmas chains. They can even be used in the making of an Advent calendar. The art circles can also be enlarged and used on murals, doors, and bulletin boards. Circles of any size can be used in many special arrangements. Use some of them to form wreaths or a Christmas tree. To form a tree, enlarge and cut out the star of the *W* page to be used on top of the tree. Use the remaining twenty-five circles to form the tree in the following way. Use one circle for the first tier, two for the second, three for the third, four for the fourth, five for the fifth, and six for the sixth. Use the last four circles, two to a row, to form the trunk.

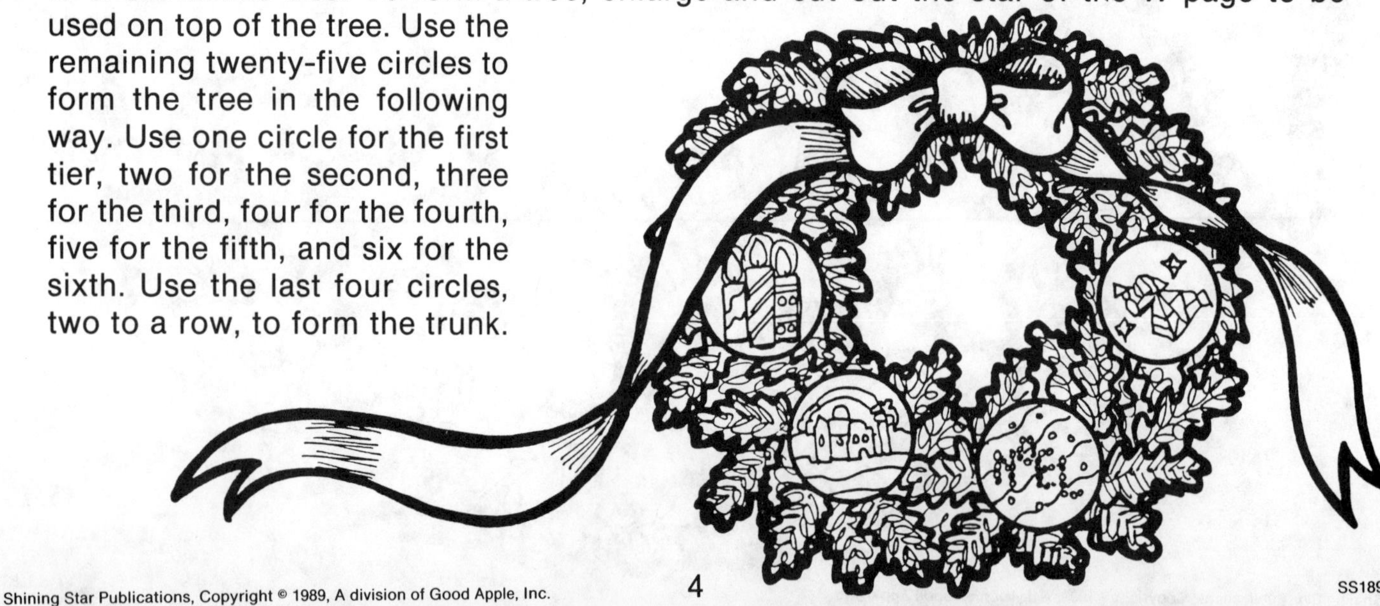

The twenty-six pages can be bound together to form books. Each child can make a complete book of crafts, or a classroom book can be made by having each child contribute one page to the book. Some pages can be mounted on plaques and used as Christmas gifts. On still other pages, the figures can be cut out of the circles and used as stick puppets or part of a Nativity scene.

To form a Nativity scene, color and cut out the patterns in this book which depict Mary, Joseph, Jesus in a manger, shepherds, kings, and a camel. Then mount them on cardboard tubes. They can also be mounted on cardboard before being cut out. Cardboard stands can be attached to them so that they can stand up. Felt can be attached to the back for flannel board stories to use with younger children.

The information given on the pages containing puzzles, games, and activity sheets can be used as suggested or incorporated into work sheets, learning centers, folder games, quizzes, etc.

DIRECTIONS FOR CIRCLE CRAFTS

A and **R**—Cover the pictures with small scraps of colored paper to form a mosaic. Since the pattern underneath won't show when covered, you do not need to use the exact shapes shown. Stay within the main outline and use any size shapes desired. If you want to make a mosaic exactly like the one pictured, trace the pieces onto thin paper. Then cut out and paste to the pattern. You can also duplicate extra patterns on sheets of colored paper. Cut out and paste onto the original pattern. Outline each piece with black marker.

B—Use watercolors to paint a sunset in the sky. Use light, bright colors to paint the mountains and sand. Paint the buildings and palm trees black to form a silhouette. An option is to make an extra copy of the picture and cut out the palm trees and buildings. The outline of the buildings and palms can then be traced onto black paper, cut out, and pasted onto the original painted background.

C—If possible, use a calligraphy pen to trace over the words *Caesar Augustus*. Color or paint the circle as desired. Cut stars out of brightly colored scraps of paper and glue them to the circle. For fun, try writing the whole *C* verse in calligraphy on a separate sheet of paper.

D,**I**,**M**, and **T**—Color the figures. Carefully cut out the figures so that the rest of the circle pattern remains intact. Cover the background by alternating strips of Christmas paper or ribbon of various patterns. Glue the figures on top of the decorated backgrounds. Use the D, I, and M pictures as a set of wall decorations, if desired. An option is to use these figures, along with the king and camel found in the *K* section of this book as part of a Nativity scene. Simply cut out the patterns, mount them on cardboard tubes, and display them against a background.

E and **O**—Use fine-point markers or sharpened pencils or crayons for these pictures. Instead of filling in the pictures with solid colors, fill in each section with dots to make a striking design. Fill in the sky and the ground with dots also.

F and **K**—Draw details onto the crowns and gifts, or add on details using gold cord, glitter, sequins, bric-a-brac, etc. Color the backgrounds and paste on a few sequins to give your finished pictures a "richer" look. The two pictures can be mounted and displayed together as matching plaques.

G—Carefully use scissors to punch a hole into each shape. Then cut out each shape without cutting into the rest of the background. Tape or glue a piece of colored tissue paper behind each hole. Hang the finished craft where light can shine through.

H—Though King Herod's heart was full of hate at the birth of Jesus, our hearts are full of various kinds of love at this time. It's also a good time to extend love to our fellow man. Cover the heart with fabric scraps to form a patchwork pattern. Then cut the letters L, O, V, and E from a piece of felt. Glue the letters onto the patchwork pattern. Your patches and letters do not have to be the same as those shown on the pattern, as the pattern will be covered anyway.

I—See directions for *D.*

J—Simply color or paint this picture. You can use it in a door greeting display, along with the other Christmas word circles found in this book (H-Love, N-Noel, and Y, for the yuletide greeting, Hope).

K—See directions for *F.*

L—First, color the background. Then roll one-inch squares of colored tissue paper into balls. Glue them onto the candle pattern. Use different colors for different parts. Allow yourself a few sessions to complete this project.

M—See directions for *D.*

N—Paint or color the background lightly so that the tiny circles can still be seen slightly. Then use a paper punch to make circles from brightly colored scraps of paper. Put a tiny dot of glue on each circle that forms the letter *N.* Cover with the colored paper circles. Use one or several colors. Repeat for each of the other letters. Then punch out circles from white paper and use them for the "snow" on the rest of the picture.

O—See directions for *E.*

P—Use markers, paints, or crayons to color this picture. The dove can be cut out, attached to a string, and used as an ornament if desired.

Q—Color the picture. Then cut pieces of yarn to glue onto Joseph's beard, and the hay. Use pieces of tissue or fabric for the head cloths and the blanket. Use sandpaper or scraps of brown wallpaper on the manger.

R—See directions for *A.*

S—Use scissors to curl strips of paper approximately one-third inch wide and three inches long. Put a dot of glue on one end of each curl and glue to the pattern. For a different effect, stand each curl on the edge instead and use rubber cement to glue it to the sheep.

T—See directions for *D.*

U—Put a circle of black construction paper behind the angel pattern and attach temporarily with masking tape. Use a pin to punch holes as indicated by the pattern through both sheets of paper. Remove the masking tape. Hang the black paper on a window or near a light source so that light can shine through the pinholes.

V—Cover this line drawing of Mary with pieces of yarn glued to each part of the outline.

W—Trace the star pattern. Cut out the traced pattern. Use it to trace the outline onto a piece of foil wrapping paper or aluminum foil. Glue onto the star in the circle. Repeat the process for each of the star's four rays. The star can also be cut out and used at the top of a paper tree.

X—Cover the picture with a circle of tracing paper. Instead of tracing the pattern with solid lines, use fine-point markers or colored pencils to write the word *CHRISTMAS* over and over again along the outline until the entire pattern has been traced. Let your project be a reminder to "Keep Christ in Christmas" and to see Christ behind all the glitter and decorations of the holiday season.

Y—Color the background. Trace the letters onto another sheet of paper and cut them out. Use the cut letters as patterns to trace onto Christmas wrapping paper. Cut and paste the wrapping paper letters over the letters on the original background.

Z—Place the pattern beneath a thin piece of solid colored material which you can see through. Use tubes of liquid embroidery to form this cross-stitch pattern. Another option is to place a piece of tracing paper on top of the pattern. Then use fine-point markers or colored pencils to trace the X's. Of course, you can also use this as a pattern for a real cross-stitch design using material and thread.

A is for *angel* Gabriel
Who told Mary she'd bear a son.
Mary *accepted* and *answered*,
"Let God's will be done."

B is the town of *Bethlehem*
Where the virgin Mary gave *birth*
To a *beautiful baby boy*
Born to save the earth.

C is for *Caesar* Augustus
Who issued a decree
For a *census* to be taken
Of every family.

D is for the *dream*
The son of *David* had one night
In which an angel warned of *danger*
And told Joseph to take flight.

E is for *Egypt*
To which the holy family fled
Till Joseph received word
That *evil* Herod was dead.

F is for *frankincense*,
A gift to the newborn king.
Gold and myrrh were the other gifts
The Magi decided to bring.

"*Glory* to *God* in the highest,"
The shepherds heard the angels say.
They spread the *good* news that the Savior
Was born for all that day.

H is for King *Herod*
Whose *heart* was full of *hate*.
The birth of the baby Jesus
Made the king irate.

I is for the crowded *inn*
Where Mary and Joseph couldn't stay.
So little *infant* Jesus was born
In a stable full of hay.

J is for *Jesus*
Who fills our hearts with *joy*,
The Son of God
And Mary's little boy.

K is for the *kings*
Who came to worship from afar.
They found the baby Jesus
By following a star.

Little baby Jesus,
You are the *light*
That guides us through the darkness
And shows us wrong from right.

M is for *Mary*,
Mother of the child
Lying in the *manger*
So tender and so *mild*.

Noel, *Noel*,
Born is a king.
He came to save us.
Rejoice and sing.

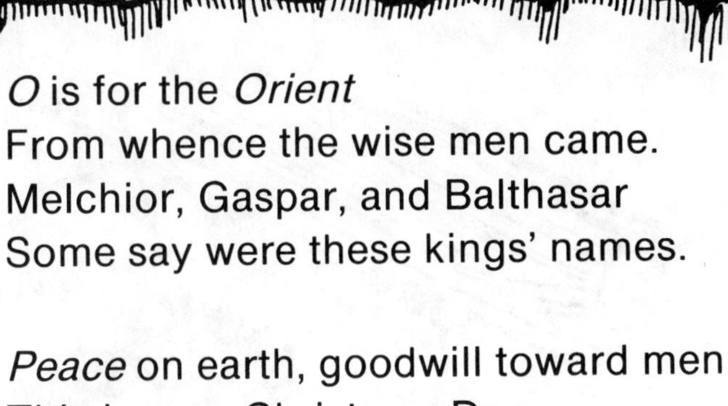

O is for the *Orient*
From whence the wise men came.
Melchior, Gaspar, and Balthasar
Some say were these kings' names.

Peace on earth, goodwill toward men
This joyous Christmas Day.
Let harmony and love *prevail*,
For this we humbly *pray.*

Q is for the *quietude*
That surrounds the manger scene,
The holy Child at its center
So peaceful and serene.

Radiant was the star that *rose*
And shone upon the earth;
The beacon guided visitors
To the place of Jesus' birth.

Some shepherds were watching their *sheep*
When an angel appeared and said
That a *Savior* wrapped in *swaddling* clothes
Could be found in a manger bed.

To terrified and *trembling* shepherds
The angel messenger said, "Fear not."
Tidings of great joy
Is what the angel brought.

"*Unto* you a child is born,"
The angel messenger said.
The shepherds made the message known
And so the news was spread.

V is for the *virgin* Mary,
So holy and so pure.
She is the mother of Jesus
And so we honor her.

W is for the *wondrous* star
Which led the *wise men* through Herod's land.
These *worshippers* returned another *way*
When *warned* of his evil plan.

X-mas is Christmas
With the word "Christ" left out,
But those who call it this
Are missing what Christmas is about.

Yuletide messages come to *you*
At Christmastime each *year*
To fill your heart with love and joy,
Gladness and good cheer.

Zacharias and Elisabeth's son, John,
Was born in ancient days.
He went before the Lord
To help prepare His ways.

A	*A* is for *angel* Gabriel Who told Mary she'd bear a son. Mary *accepted* and *answered*, "Let God's will be done."

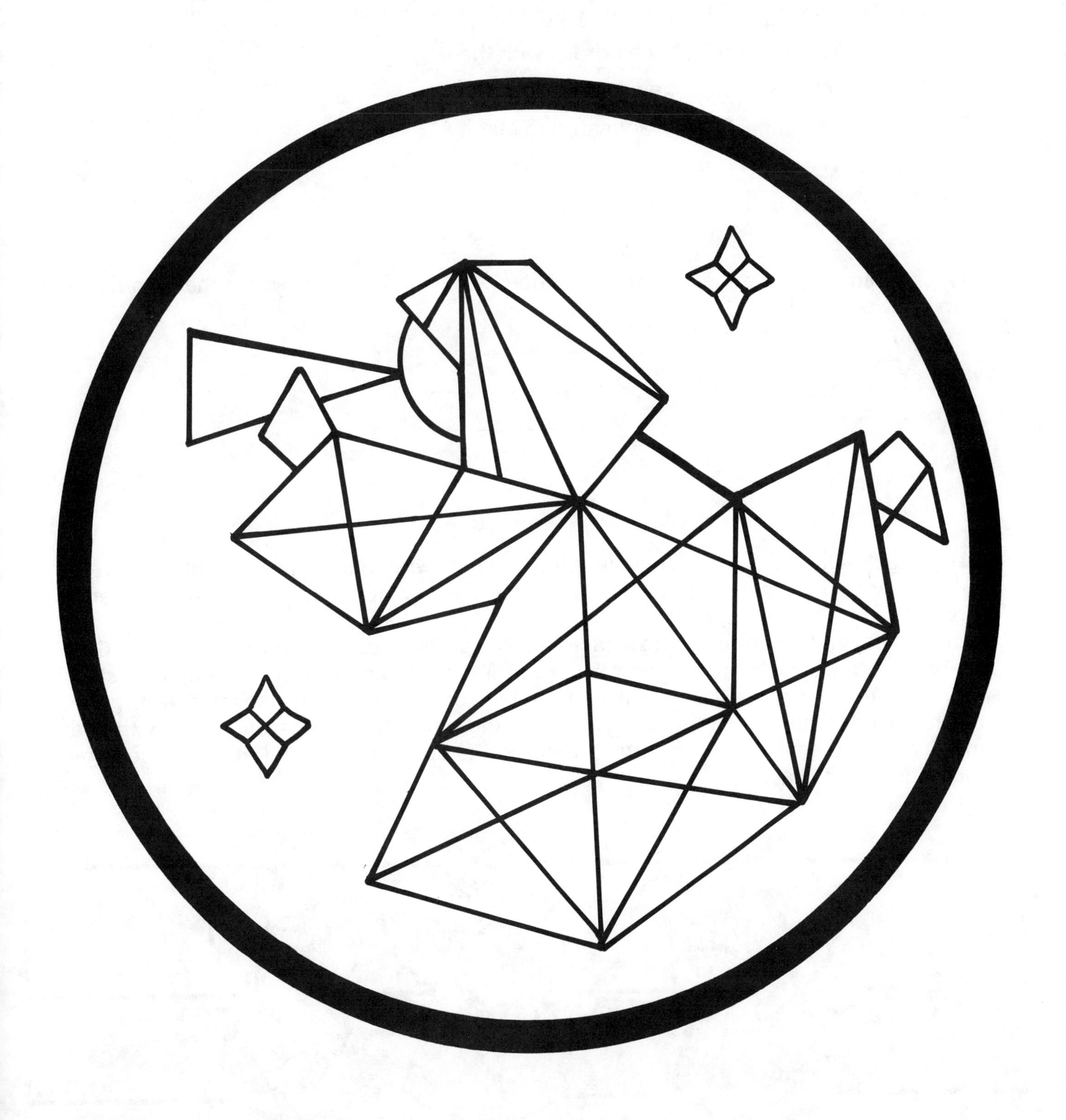

A is for *Angel* Gabriel
Who told Mary she'd bear a son.
Mary *accepted* and *answered*,
"Let God's will be done."

Arranging Sentences—Arrange these sentences in the correct order by numbering them one to six.

1. _______ The angel told Mary she would give birth to Jesus.
2. _______ The angel said, "The Lord is with thee . . . ."
3. _______ Mary wondered how she could bear a son.
4. _______ The angel Gabriel appeared to Mary.
5. _______ The angel Gabriel left.
6. _______ Mary told the angel she agreed to God's plan.

Anagrams—Rearrange the letters of the given words to form words that can be found in the Nativity story.

ARMY	1. ____________
FILED	2. ____________
ARTS	3. ____________
GLEAN	4. ____________
SEAT	5. ____________

Art Angel—Decorate a paper cone with garland, wrapping paper, ribbon, etc. Near the narrow part of the cone, punch two holes directly opposite one another. Insert a short pipe cleaner through the holes and bend it to look like arms. Cut a circle out of heavy paper for the face. Draw facial features and glue on yarn for the hair. Glue the head to a Popsicle stick. Snip off the tip of the cone and insert the Popsicle stick. Tape or glue into place. Use a wire egg holder or a pipe cleaner covered with glitter and bend into shape for the halo. Attach to the cone. Cut wings out of heavy paper and decorate them with glitter. Attach them to the cone and you will have a nice angel decoration to display.

A B C

ALPHABET BIBLICAL CONNECTION GAME

Directions: The first person says a word beginning with *A*. All words for the game must come from either the first or second chapters of the Gospel according to Luke or the first or second chapters of the Gospel according to Matthew. The word, *angel* for example, can be used to start the game. The first person then thinks of a word which begins with the last letter of *angel*. This person does not say the word out loud, but gives a clue pertaining to the word. The next person must guess the word within a specified amount of time. If it cannot be guessed, the clue is given to the next person. Any person who cannot guess the word or who cannot think of a clue for the next person is out. The winner is the last person left. A sample round is given below. It can be used as a written activity for practice.

1. A name for God __________
2. Joseph received a warning during one of these. __________
3. One of the wise men's gifts __________
4. "Glory to God in the ________." __________
5. "I bring you good ________ of great joy." __________
6. They were watching their flock. __________
7. The relationship of Jesus to Mary __________
8. The town where Jesus grew up __________
9. An evil king __________
10. Bethlehem is called the city of ________. __________

After one round has been played, start a new round. This time use a word beginning with *B*. Vary the game by using words, but no clues, or select a theme other than Christmas. A round using books of the Bible, for example, might include words in the following order:

JUD**E**, **E**ZEKIE**L**, **L**UK**E**, **E**STHE**R**, **R**EVELATIO**N**, **N**EHEMIA**H**, **H**AGGA**I**, **I**SAIA**H**, **H**ABAKKU**K**, **K**ING**S**, **S**AMUE**L**, **L**AMENTATION**S**, **S**OLOMON'S SON**G**, **G**ALATIANS

B

B is the town of *Bethlehem*
Where the virgin Mary gave *birth*
To a *beautiful baby boy*
Born to save the earth.

B is the town of *Bethlehem*
Where the virgin Mary gave *birth*
To a *beautiful baby boy*
Born to save the earth.

*B*ethlehem Blanks—Fill in the puzzle with the answer to each clue.

B _ _ _ _ _ _ _ _	Christmas is the _ of Jesus.
E _ _ _ _	Jesus was born upon the _ to save mankind.
T _ _ _ _	Traditionally the number of wise men bringing gifts to Jesus is _.
H _ _ _	Mary, Joseph, and Jesus are called the _ family.
L _ _ _ _	Jesus is sometimes called the _ of the World.
E _ _ _ _	The holy family fled to _ to escape from Herod.
H _ _ _ _	_ wanted the baby Jesus killed.
E _ _ _	The wise men came from lands in the _.
M _ _ _	The wise men are also called the _.

*B*irthday Balloons—Celebrate the birthday of Jesus by writing Christmas messages on thin strips of paper. Insert the messages into balloons and fill them with helium. Release them and let the joy of Christ's birth be spread.

*B*ookmarks—Make bookmarks out of heavy paper. Decorate them with Christmas symbols, such as a star, the town of Bethlehem, baby Jesus, or a crown. Use the patterns below or design your own.

BETHLEHEM MATCH GAME

Directions: Color the cards. Mount them on cardboard. Cut the cards apart. Mix them up and place them face down in front of you. Find one or two other players to play this game with you. The first player turns over two cards. If a matching picture and verse are turned over, the player keeps the pair and gets another turn. If the two cards do not match, turn them face down again. Then it is the next player's turn. Continue to play until all the cards have been matched. The player with the most cards wins.

"Now when Jesus was born in Bethlehem of Judaea in the days of Herod the king, behold, there came *wise men* from the east to Jerusalem."
Matthew 2:1

"And Joseph also went up from Galilee, out of the city of Nazareth, into Judaea, unto the city of David, which is called *Bethlehem*; . . ."
Luke 2:4

"And this shall be a sign unto you; Ye shall find the *babe* wrapped in swaddling clothes, lying in a manger."
Luke 2:12

"And there were in the same country *shepherds* abiding in the field, keeping watch over their flock by night."
Luke 2:8

"And the *angel* said unto them, Fear not: for, behold, I bring you good tidings of great joy, which shall be to all people."
Luke 2:10

"When they saw the *star*, they rejoiced with exceeding great joy."
Matthew 2:10

"And they came with haste, and found *Mary*, and *Joseph*, and the *babe* lying in a manger."
Luke 2:16

". . . and when they had opened their treasures, they presented unto him *gifts*; gold, and frankincense, and myrrh."
Matthew 2:11

C

C is for *Caesar* Augustus
Who issued a decree
For a *census* to be taken
Of every family.

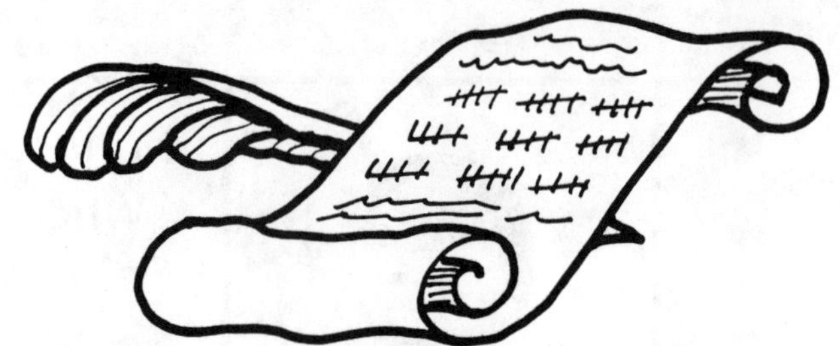

C is for *Caesar* Augustus
Who issued a decree
For a *census* to be taken
Of every family.

*C*rossword Puzzle—All the answers to this crossword puzzle begin with *C*. Write the answers to the given clues.

Across
1. Bethlehem is called the ___ of David.
3. Mary wrapped Jesus in swaddling ___.
4. The Roman emperor at the time of Christ's birth was ___ Augustus.

Down
1. The shepherds found the Christ ___ lying in a manger.
2. A ___ is a count.

*C*ensus—Count the people in this picture puzzle. Write your answer here. ______

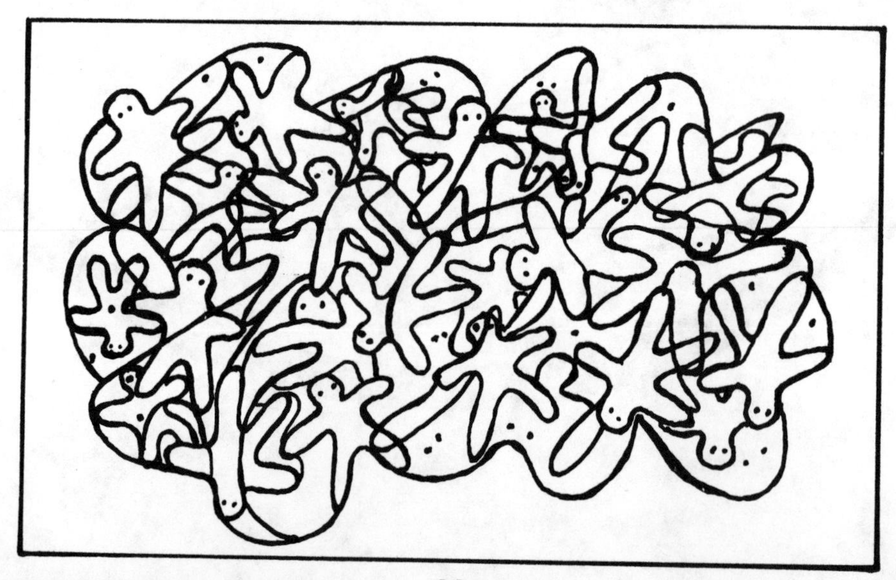

CHRISTMAS CAROL CHARADES

Directions: Cut out the slips of paper and put them in a box. Divide the group into two teams. The first person on Team One picks out a slip of paper. Using only motions, this person tries to get teammates to guess the Christmas carols listed. If this can successfully be done in under two minutes, the team scores points. The number of points scored equals the number of words in the title of the Christmas carol. Teams take turns acting out the charades. Younger children may need to see a list of the carols ahead of time. Keep score for the ten rounds on Caesar's Official Count Card.

AWAY IN A MANGER
ANGELS WE HAVE HEARD ON HIGH
THE FIRST NOEL
GOD REST YE MERRY, GENTLEMEN
HARK! THE HERALD ANGELS SING
I SAW THREE SHIPS
IT CAME UPON A MIDNIGHT CLEAR
JOY TO THE WORLD
LET THERE BE PEACE ON EARTH
O COME, ALL YE FAITHFUL
O COME, O COME, EMMANUEL
O HOLY NIGHT
O LITTLE TOWN OF BETHLEHEM
SILENT NIGHT
WE THREE KINGS
WHAT CHILD IS THIS
I HEARD THE BELLS ON CHRISTMAS DAY
DO YOU HEAR WHAT I HEAR?
LITTLE DRUMMER BOY
GO, TELL IT ON THE MOUNTAIN

CAESAR'S OFFICIAL COUNT CARD

											TOTAL
TEAM 1											
TEAM 2											

D

D is for the *dream*
The son of *David* had one night
In which an angel warned of *danger*
And told Joseph to take flight.

D is for the *dream*
The son of *David* had one night
In which an angel warned of *danger*
And told Joseph to take flight.

*D*ot-to-Dot—Connect the dots to find something the family used that begins with a *D*. Write what it is here. ___________

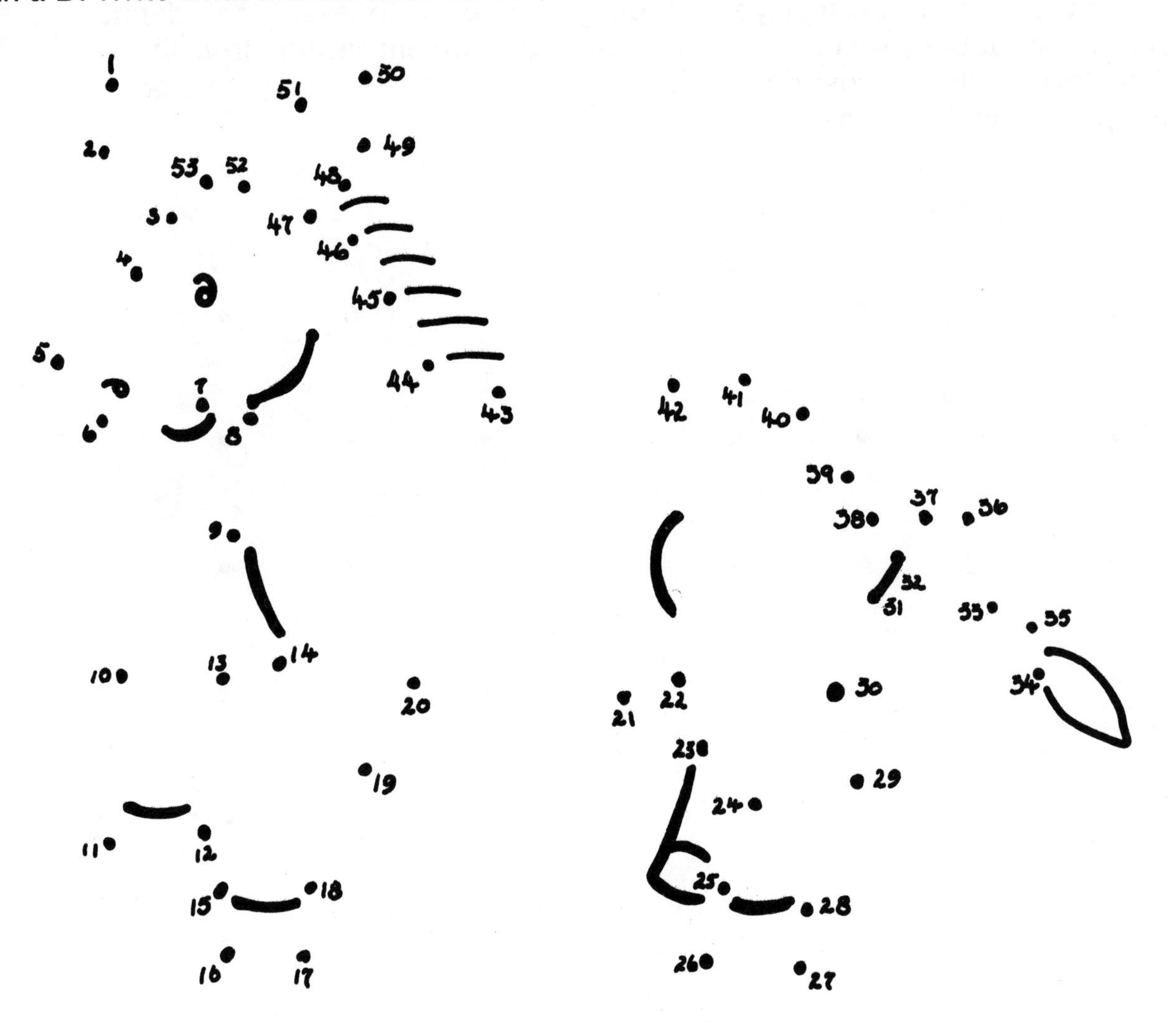

*D*ream Drawing—Draw a picture of one of your dreams. Tell about it.

DOT DANGER

Directions: This game is for two players. Player One draws a line between two vertical or horizontal dots. Then Player Two takes a turn. The player who connects the dots that complete the square may initial the square and take another turn. Several turns in a row may be taken as long as the player keeps completing squares. The object of the game is to try to make as many squares as possible with the exception of those containing the letters in the word DANGER. After all the dots have been connected, scores are tallied by each player. Players get one point for every "non-dangerous" square. They must subtract two points for every square containing a letter from the word DANGER. The player with the most points wins. This game can also be drawn on the blackboard and played by two teams.

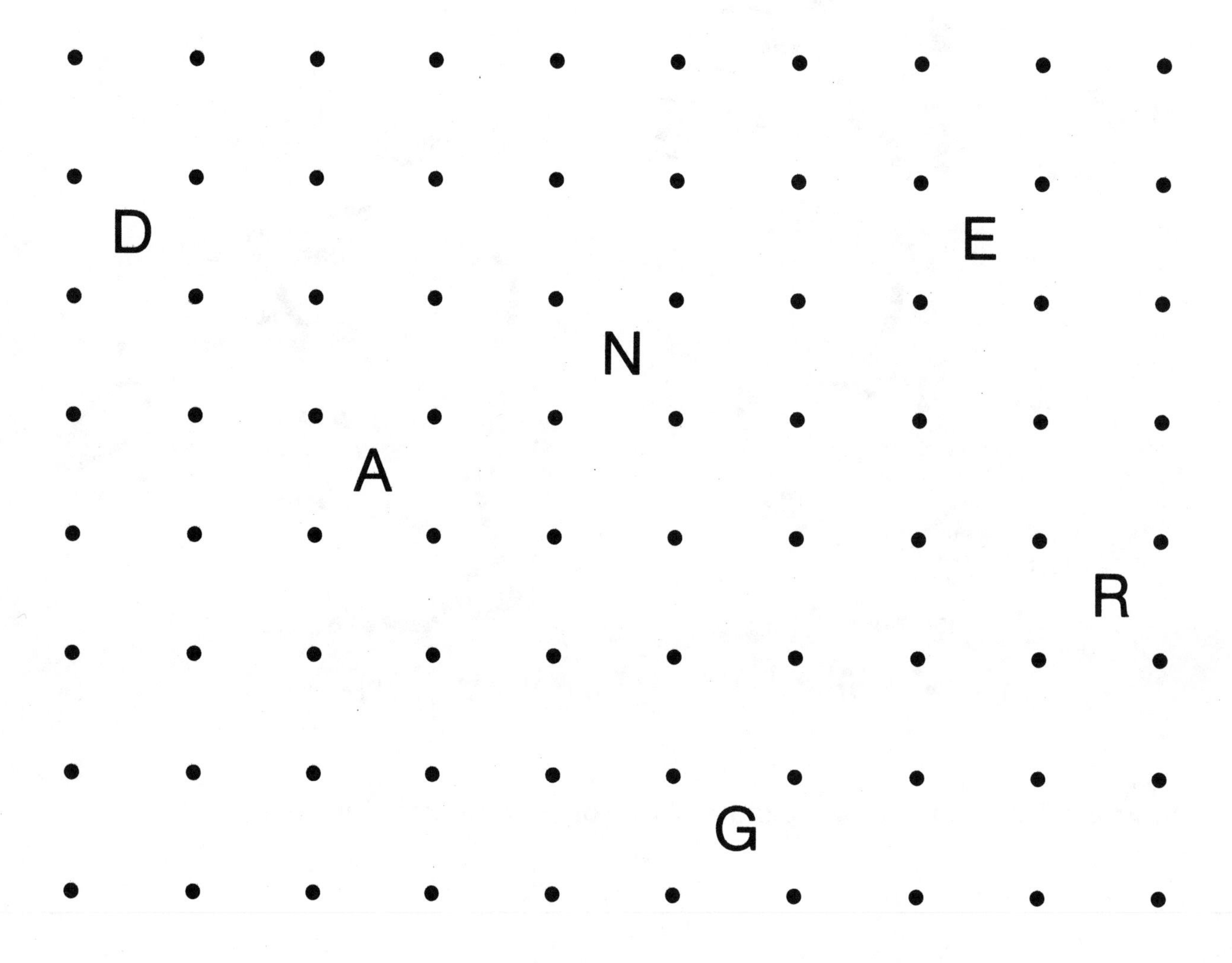

E	*E* is for *Egypt* To which the holy family fled Till Joseph received word That *evil* Herod was dead.

E is for *Egypt*
To which the holy family fled
Till Joseph received word
That *evil* Herod was dead.

*E*nvelope Exchange—Find pictures of the Nativity story on used Christmas cards. Cut each one into puzzle pieces. Put each puzzle in a separate envelope. Exchange envelopes with a friend and solve each other's puzzles.

*E*nlarge a Picture—Enlarge the given picture of the family fleeing to Egypt by copying what is in each small square and drawing an enlarged version of it in the corresponding large square.

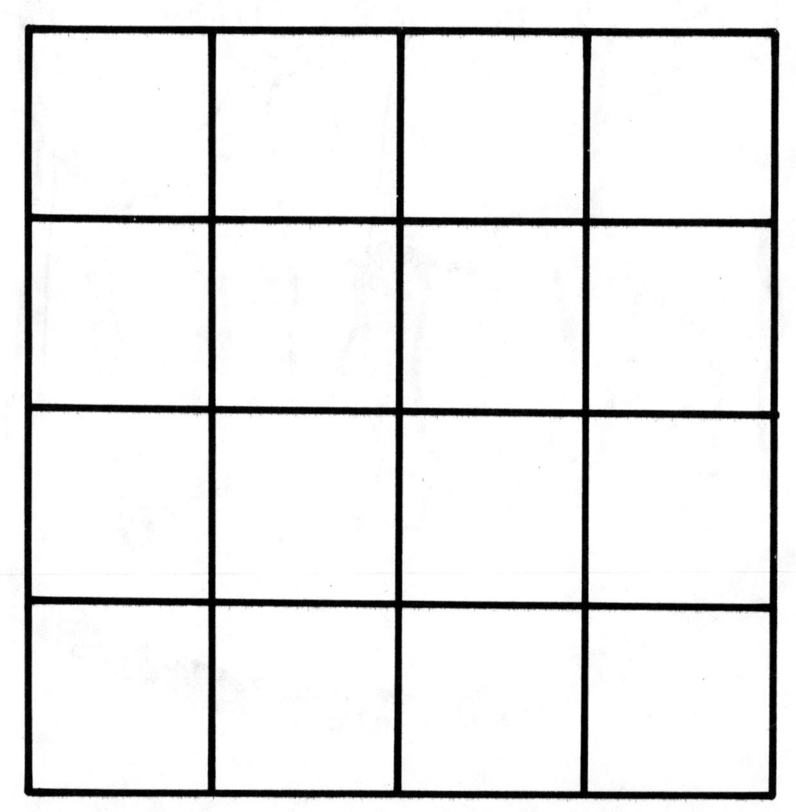

ELIMINATION GAME

Directions: This page can be used as an activity sheet or as a game. To play the game, each child will need two Popsicle sticks or tongue depressors. Have the children make a donkey and a sheep to represent two animals taditionally associated with the Nativity story. Put a *T* for true on the donkey and an *F* for false on the sheep. Attach each animal to a stick. All children should stand. The first statement should be read. Allow children to decide upon an answer. Then say, True or False. Children must then raise their answers immediately. Those answering incorrectly must sit down, but they may participate in the game from their seats. Repeat the process for all twenty questions. The last child out wins. If all questions have been used and several children remain standing, they can all be declared winners or your own challenge questions may be asked.

1. The Gospel according to Luke tells about the Nativity. __________
2. Mary stayed with Elisabeth for about three months. __________
3. An angel appeared to the wise men and told them of Christ's birth. __________
4. King Herod issued a decree that all the world should be taxed. __________
5. The Bible says that three wise men visited the baby Jesus. __________
6. Joseph was of the house of David. __________
7. The Bible says Jesus was born on December 25th. __________
8. Jesus was Mary's firstborn son. __________
9. Emmanuel means Savior. __________
10. In the Bible, Mark tells about the birth of Jesus. __________
11. Joseph and Mary went to Nazareth to be taxed. __________
12. Angels appeared to the shepherds saying, "Joy to the world." __________
13. The wise men spoke of Jesus as the King of the Jews. __________
14. King Herod rejoiced at the news of Christ's birth. __________
15. Bethlehem was in Galilee. __________
16. The angel Gabriel told Mary she would have a son. __________
17. The names of the wise men are listed in the Bible. __________
18. Joseph was warned in a dream to flee to Egypt. __________
19. The shepherds were frightened when they first saw the angel. __________
20. The wise men visited Herod after they saw the baby Jesus. __________

F	*F* is for *frankincense*, A gift to the newborn king. Gold and myrrh were the other gifts The Magi decided to bring.

F is for *frankincense*,
A gift to the newborn king.
Gold and myrrh were the other gifts
The Magi decided to bring.

*F*ill-Ins—Find a word in the above poem which is most clearly related to each given word and fill it in the blank.

1. Present ______________
2. Majesty ______________
3. Wise men ______________
4. Carry ______________
5. Metal ______________

*F*lannel Board Felt Figures—Cut and glue pieces of felt together to make Nativity scene figures similar to the ones below. Use the finished figures and a flannel board to tell the story of the Nativity.

FIND THE GIFTS

Directions: This game is for two players. Both players write the words GOLD, FRANKINCENSE, and MYRRH somewhere on their first grid. Words must be written vertically or horizontally with only one letter per space. The first player begins by calling out a space designated by a letter and a number (such as E-7). If the space called out contains a letter, the other player must say what gift was found, but does not tell what letter was found. If the space does not contain a letter, the player simply says, "You missed." After one guess, it is the other player's turn to guess. Each player should keep track of correct guesses with an *O* and incorrect ones with an *X*. When a player has found an entire gift, he or she should be told. The first player to completely find all three gifts wins.

G	"*Glory* to *God* in the highest," The shepherds heard the angels say. They spread the *good* news that the Savior Was born for all that day.

"*G*lory to *God* in the highest,"
The shepherds heard the angels say.
They spread the *good* news that the Savior
Was born for all that day.

*G*reeting Card—Make a greeting card to spread the good news of Jesus' birth.

*G*ood Deed Gifts—Use colored paper to make paper packages like the ones below. On the back of each gift write a good deed that you will do for someone. Write who the good deed gift is for and who it is from on paper gift tags.

GO SEARCH FOR GOOD NEWS

Directions: Write the following words on flashcards: women, thee, highest, Jacob, end, impossible, joy, David, peace and men. Hide the flashcards around the room so that only a small portion of each card is showing. Also hide ten blank flashcards to make the game a little harder. Divide the group into two teams. Read the first statement out loud. The first player on each team has thirty seconds to hunt for the answer. As the players find cards, they must not indicate what words are on the cards. Neither may they indicate that a card is blank. After looking at a card, they must immediately return it to its hiding place. (Players waiting their turns will notice some of the hiding places, but will not know what is on each card.) When a player thinks he/she has found the correct answer, the card is held up and the answer read out loud. Each player is allowed only one guess during the thirty second time period. Players guessing correctly keep the cards for their teams. If the first player on each team cannot find the answer within thirty seconds, the second player on each team gets a chance, then the third, etc. until the correct answer has been found. The next players are then given a new statement to complete. The team holding the most cards after all ten have been found is the winning team.

As a variation of the game, do not write the answers on flashcards. Instead, let children use their Bibles (Luke 1-2) to find the answers. The first person to find a correct answer scores a point for that team.

This page can also be used as a Bible work sheet. You may want to award a Christmas prize to the first person who completes it correctly.

WHAT GOOD NEWS DID THE ANGELS BRING?

1. ". . . blessed art thou among ____________."
2. ". . . the Lord is with ____________: . . ."
3. "He shall be great, and shall be called the Son of the ____________: . . ."
4. "And he shall reign over the house of ____________ for ever; . . ."
5. ". . . and of his kingdom there shall be no ____________."
6. "For with God nothing shall be ____________."
7. " . . . Fear not: for, behold, I bring you good tidings of great ____________, . . ."
8. "For unto you is born this day in the city of ____________ a Saviour, which is Christ the Lord."
9. "Glory to God in the highest, and on earth ____________, . . ."
10. ". . . good will toward ____________."

H	*H* is for King *Herod* Whose *heart* was full of *hate*. The birth of the baby Jesus Made the king irate.

H is for King *Herod*
Whose *heart* was full of *hate*.
The birth of the baby Jesus
Made the king irate.

*H*andmade Cards—Draw a picture of Mary, Joseph, or Jesus on the front of a card. Write a prayer on the back. Share with others.

*H*idden Pictures—Mary, Joseph, and Jesus had to hide from Herod's soldiers because Herod wanted the newborn king put to death. Find Mary, Joseph, and Jesus hidden in the picture. Circle them.

HOLY FAMILY GAME

Directions: This game is for two or three players. Each player chooses a marker and places it near "Start." The first player rolls one die and moves the number of spaces indicated by the die. Then the other players take turns. Players must follow any directions marked on the spaces in which they land. The first player to land on finish wins. (An exact roll of the die is not needed to win.)

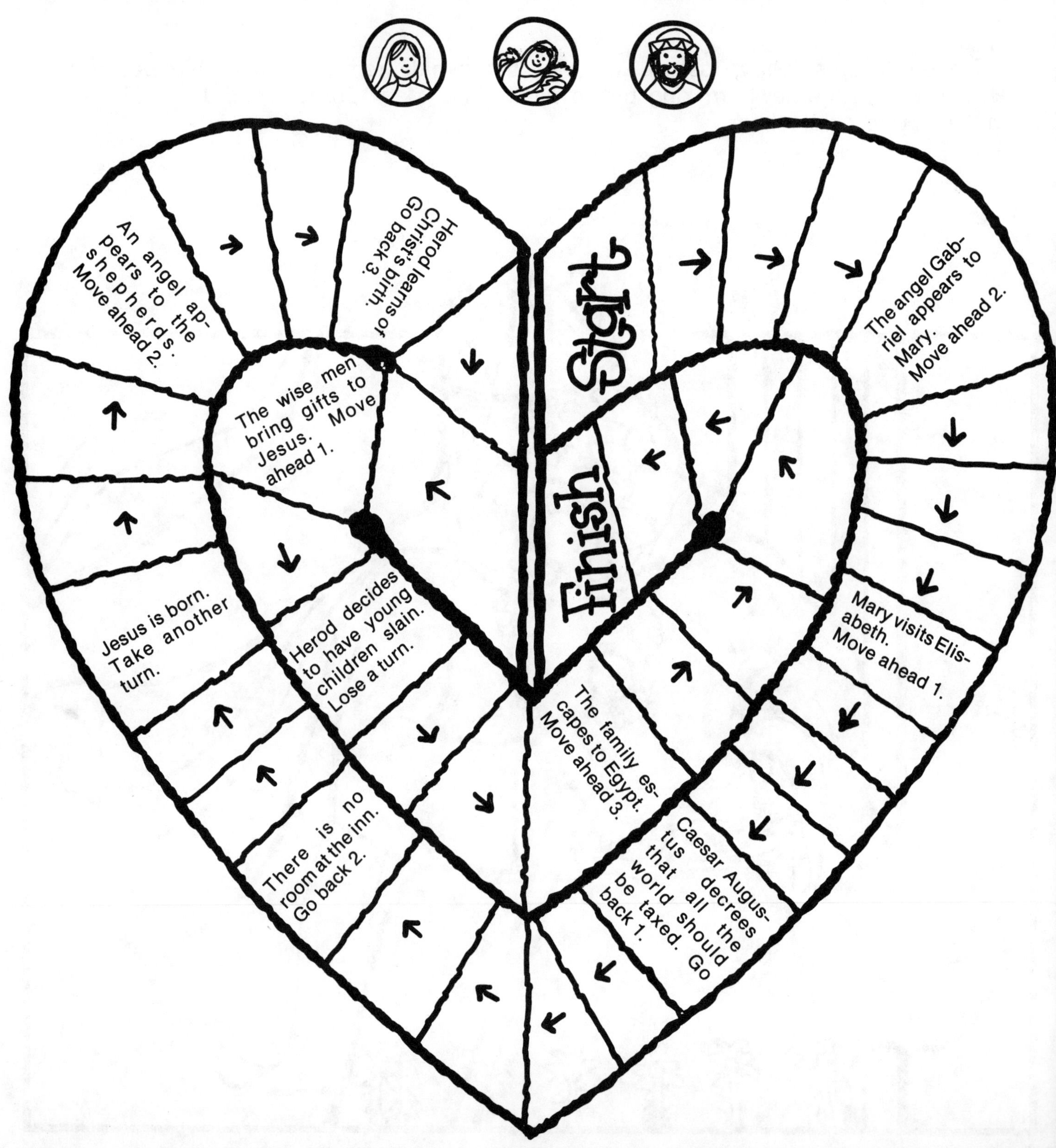

I

I is for the crowded *inn*
Where Mary and Joseph couldn't stay.
So little *infant* Jesus was born
In a stable full of hay.

I is for the crowded *inn*
Where Mary and Joseph couldn't stay.
So little *infant* Jesus was born
In a stable full of hay.

Imagination Activities—Imagine the place where Jesus was born. What do you see and hear? Write about some of the things you imagined.

Now imagine how different the birth would have been if Jesus was born in one of today's modern hotels or hospitals. Write about some of the things you imagined.

Illustration—Illustrate the part of the Christmas story in which the innkeeper tells Joseph there is no room left at the inn.

IN THE INN

Directions: Players take turns tossing a coin at the "inn." If the coin touches a space not occupied by another player's initials (or team number if teams are playing), the player may write his/her inititals (or team number) inside the "room." After all the rooms have been filled, count up the number of rooms occupied by each person or team to determine the winner(s). Use a pencil to write inside the rooms so that the initials can be erased for a new game. The gameboard can also be enlarged and laminated. Then, overhead markers or grease pencils can be used.

J	*J* is for *Jesus* Who fills our hearts with *joy*, The Son of God And Mary's little boy.

J is for *Jesus*
Who fills our hearts with *joy*,
The Son of God
And Mary's little boy.

*J*umbled Words—Rearrange each set of given letters to spell a word which can be used to refer to Jesus.

1. STRICH ____________________
2. AVORIS ____________________
3. DREEMERE ____________________
4. OLDR ____________________
5. LANEMUME ____________________
6. GINK ____________________
7. FINTAN ____________________
8. SAMEHIS ____________________
9. ONS ____________________
10. GILTH ____________________

*J*oyful News—Find and circle the following joyful words which are hidden in the picture: hope, love, joy, cheer and merry.

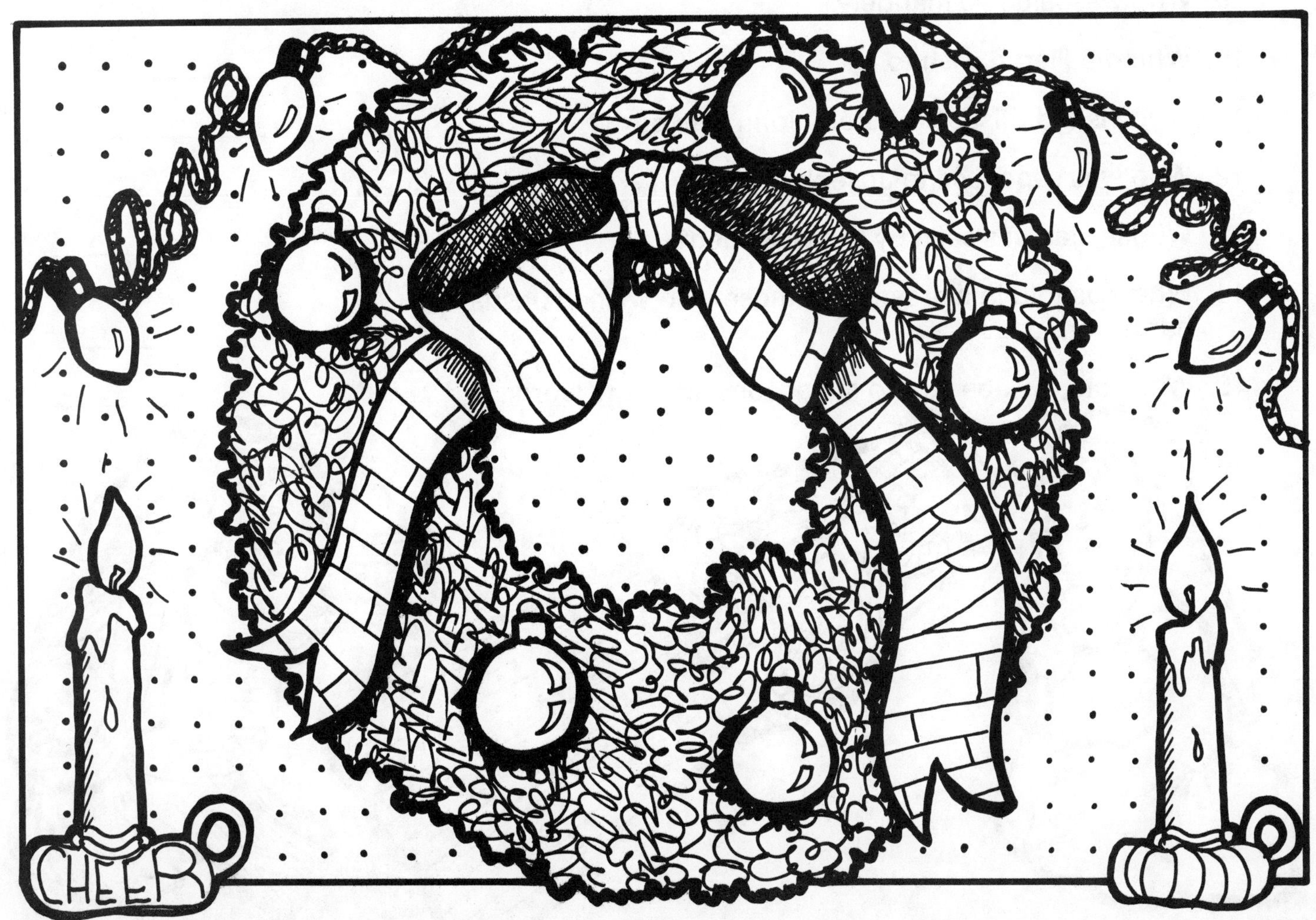

JESUS, MARY, AND JOSEPH GAME

Directions: Color and cut out the figures below and glue them to wooden sticks. Read the questions to the players. After each question say, "Who's Who?" At that point, players raise one of the characters as an answer. Any player raising the incorrect character is out of the game. The last player left (or anyone left at the end of the questions) wins. This page can also be used as an activity sheet to be completed by each person.

1. Who did the wise men refer to as the King of the Jews? ____________
2. Whose birth troubled King Herod? ____________
3. Who said, "My soul doth magnify the Lord"? ____________
4. Who did the angel Gabriel greet saying, . . "Hail, thou art highly favoured, the Lord is with thee: . . ."? ____________
5. Who was warned in a dream to flee to Egypt? ____________
6. Who said, ". . . from henceforth all generations shall call me blessed"? ____________
7. Who is called Emmanuel? ____________
8. Who said, ". . . How shall this be, seeing I know not a man?" ____________
9. Who was laid in a manger? ____________
10. Who did Herod wish to kill? ____________
11. Who visited Elisabeth before John was born? ____________
12. Who was espoused to Joseph? ____________
13. Whose star was seen by the wise men? ____________
14. Who was told in a dream that those who wished Jesus harm were dead? ____________
15. Who said, ". . . be it unto me according to thy word . . . ."? ____________

K	*K* is for the *kings* Who came to worship from afar. They found the baby Jesus By following a star.

Wise Man
Wise Man
Wise Man

K is for the *kings*
Who came to worship from afar.
They found the baby Jesus
By following a star.

Kingly Knowledge—Circle three correct answers for each question.

1. Which of these have been used to refer to those who came from the east to Bethlehem to worship Jesus?

   A. Magi B. astrologers C. wise men D. shepherds

2. Which of these names have traditionally been given them?

   A. Melchior B. Pilate C. Balthasar D. Gaspar

3. Which gifts were brought by the kings?

   A. frankincense B. copper C. myrrh D. gold

Kitchen Craft Kings—Cut an oval out of poster board to be used as a king's face. Add features with items found in your kitchen. Use any materials available. For example, you could make a macaroni beard, spaghetti hair, an aluminum foil crown, a pipe cleaner mouth, bottlecap eyes, etc. You may wish to spray paint some items before gluing them to the king's face.

Kings Three—Take one set of letters from each crown to form a word. For example, the letter combinations JU, DE, and A from the three crowns form the word JUDEA. Do the same to form ten other words. Write them in the given blanks.

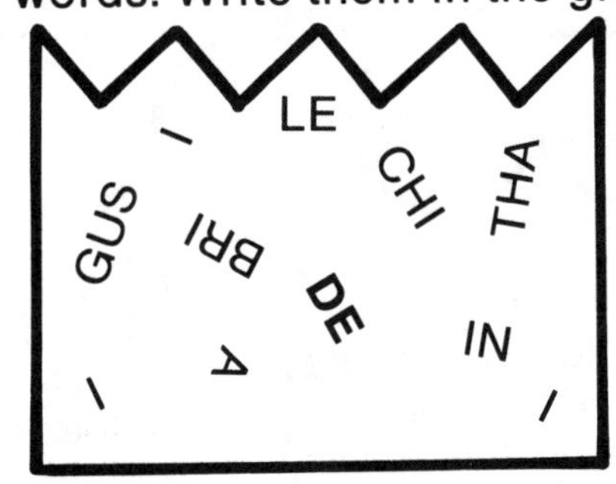

RETH
LEE
OR
SAR
A
CENSE
EL
A
TUDE
HEM
TUS

_______________ _______________

_______________ _______________

_______________ _______________

_______________ _______________

_______________ _______________

KING'S RACE

Directions: Cut out the pieces very carefully. Have a race against other players to match up the pieces to form crowns. Match each king's name to his description. You will know you are right if the pieces fit properly. The first person to put all the crowns together is the winner. Optional—After you practice several days, have someone quiz you by giving you each king's description out loud. You must write down the name that goes with each clue.

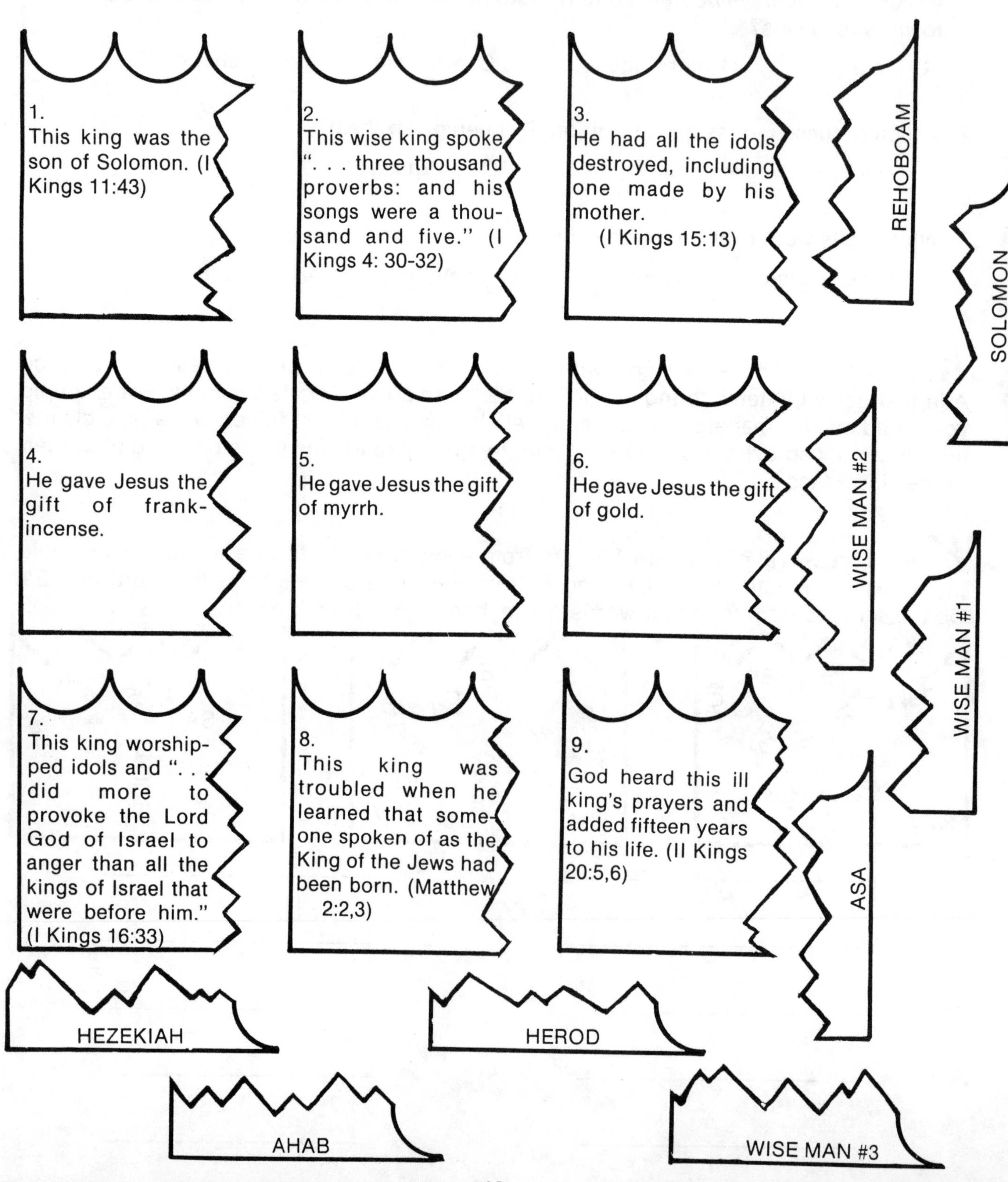

L

Little baby Jesus,
You are the *light*
That guides us through the darkness
And shows us wrong from right.

Little baby Jesus,
You are the *light*
That guides us through the darkness
And shows us wrong from right.

Little Light—On black construction paper, draw a simple picture of the baby Jesus lying in a manger. You may wish to use the one below for a pattern. Next use a straight pin to punch holes along your drawing. Punching the holes too far apart will make the picture unrecognizable. Punching the holes too close together may cause the paper to tear. When you are finished, hang the black paper near a source of light. The light will shine through the holes to show that Jesus is the Light of the World.

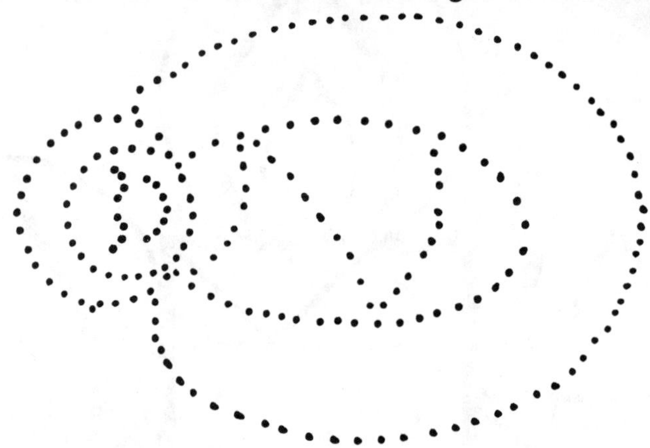

Letter—Write a letter to the baby Jesus. If it were deliverable anywhere, how would you address the envelope? Use the space below for your letter. Then use the envelope drawing to show how you would address it.

____

____

____

____

____

____

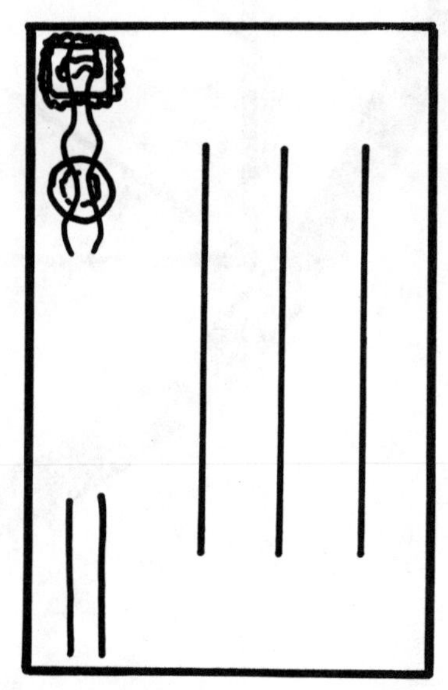

LIFE OF JESUS LINK-UPS

Directions: Each child needs twenty strips of colored paper. Each time the teacher reads a clue, the player writes an answer on a strip of paper. Every time a player gets a correct answer, it may be linked to that players other correct answers to form a chain. The winner is the one with the most chain links connected. Players may wish to hang their chains of knowledge.

This game can also be played by teams. The teacher reads a clue to the first player on each team. The first player to answer correctly may write the answer on a strip of paper and use it as part of a team chain. Then the teacher reads a clue to the next player on each team. After all the clues have been read, the team with the most links is the winning team.

This page can also be used as a fill-in activity sheet.

1. He was born in ______________.
2. His mother was named ______________.
3. King ______________ was troubled by His birth.
4. The ______________ gave Him gifts of gold, frankincense and myrrh.
5. His family fled into ______________ to save Him from Herod's evil plan.
6. When He was twelve, Mary and Joseph found Him in the ______________ amazing all with His understanding.
7. He grew up in the city of ______________.
8. He was baptized by ______________.
9. Before He began His ministry, the ______________ promised Him all the kingdoms of the world.
10. He chose men like Simon and Andrew to be His ______________.
11. He performed His first miracle at a wedding feast in ______________.
12. Jesus drove the moneychangers from the ______________.
13. With a few loaves and ______________ Jesus was able to feed a multitude of people.
14. When Jesus entered the city of ______________, the people cried, "Hosanna . . . Blessed is he that cometh in the name of the Lord; . . ."
15. Jesus often taught using stories called ______________.
16. Jesus celebrated the feast of the ______________ with His disciples.
17. ______________ betrayed Jesus with a kiss.
18. Jesus was taken to Pontius ______________ to be tried.
19. Jesus was scourged, then crowned with ______________.
20. Jesus was crucified on a ______________.

M

M is for *Mary*,
Mother of the child
Lying in the *manger*
So tender and so *mild*.

M is for *Mary*,
Mother of the child
Lying in the *manger*
So tender and so *mild*.

*M*anger Mobile—Make a mobile of the characters you would find in a manger scene.

*M*aze—Help visitors find their way to the baby Jesus.

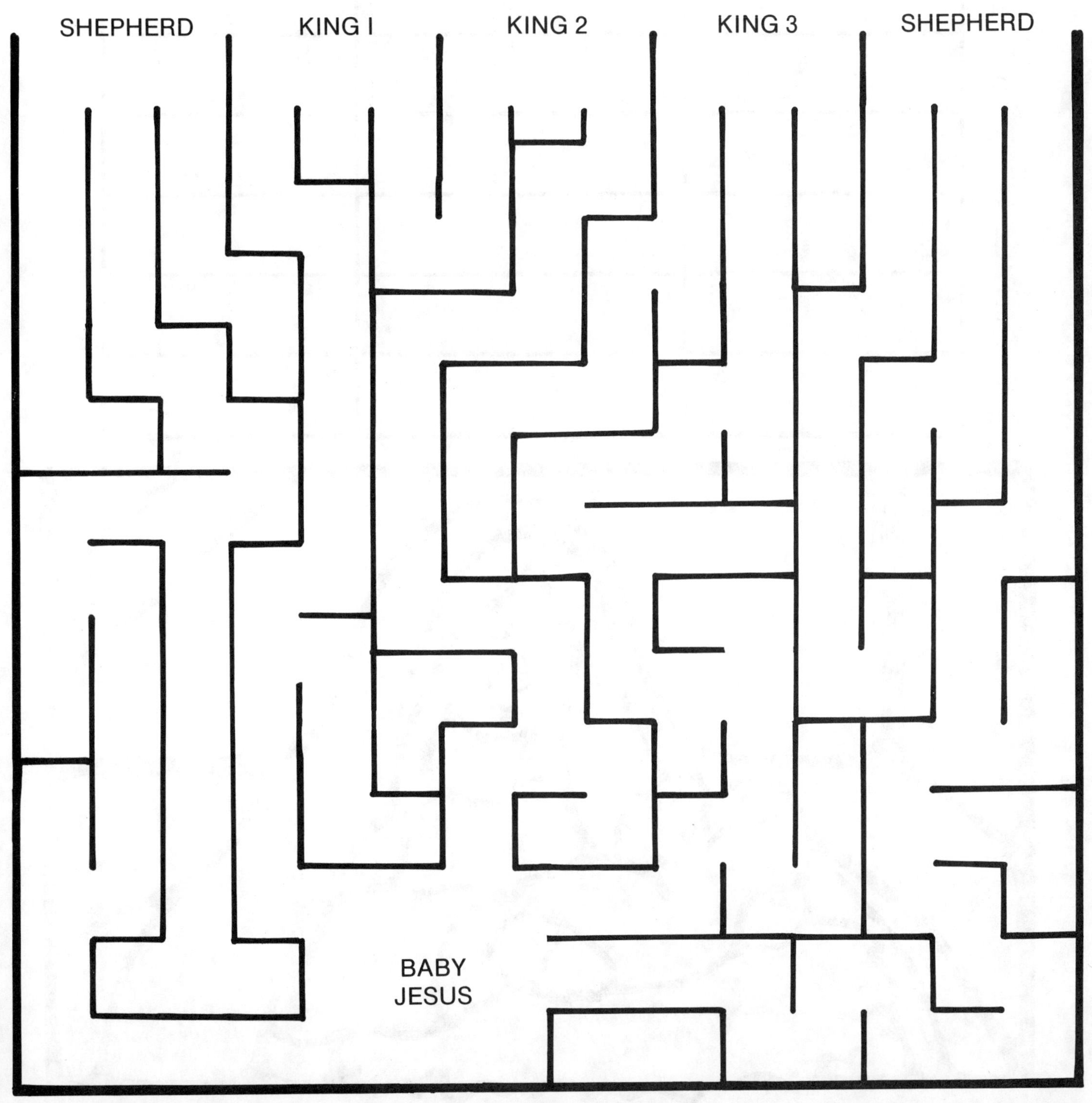

MARY, THE MOTHER OF JESUS

Directions: Fill in the chart with words beginning with the letters and categories indicated. Use your Bible for help. Try to be the first person or team to complete the entire chart.

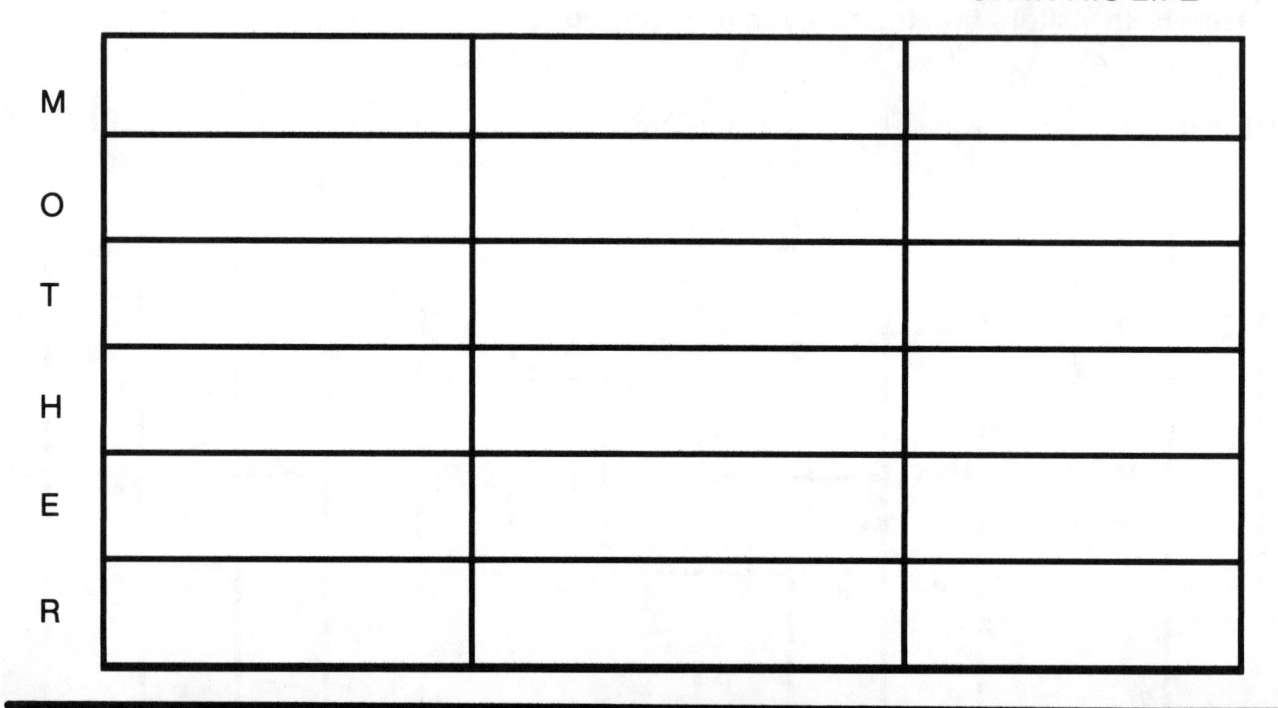

	A BOOK OF THE BIBLE	A PLACE MENTIONED IN THE BIBLE	SOMEONE IN THE GENEALOGY OF JESUS (MATTHEW 1) OR IN HIS LIFE
M			
O			
T			
H			
E			
R			

N

Noel, Noel,
Born is a king.
He came to save us.
Rejoice and sing.

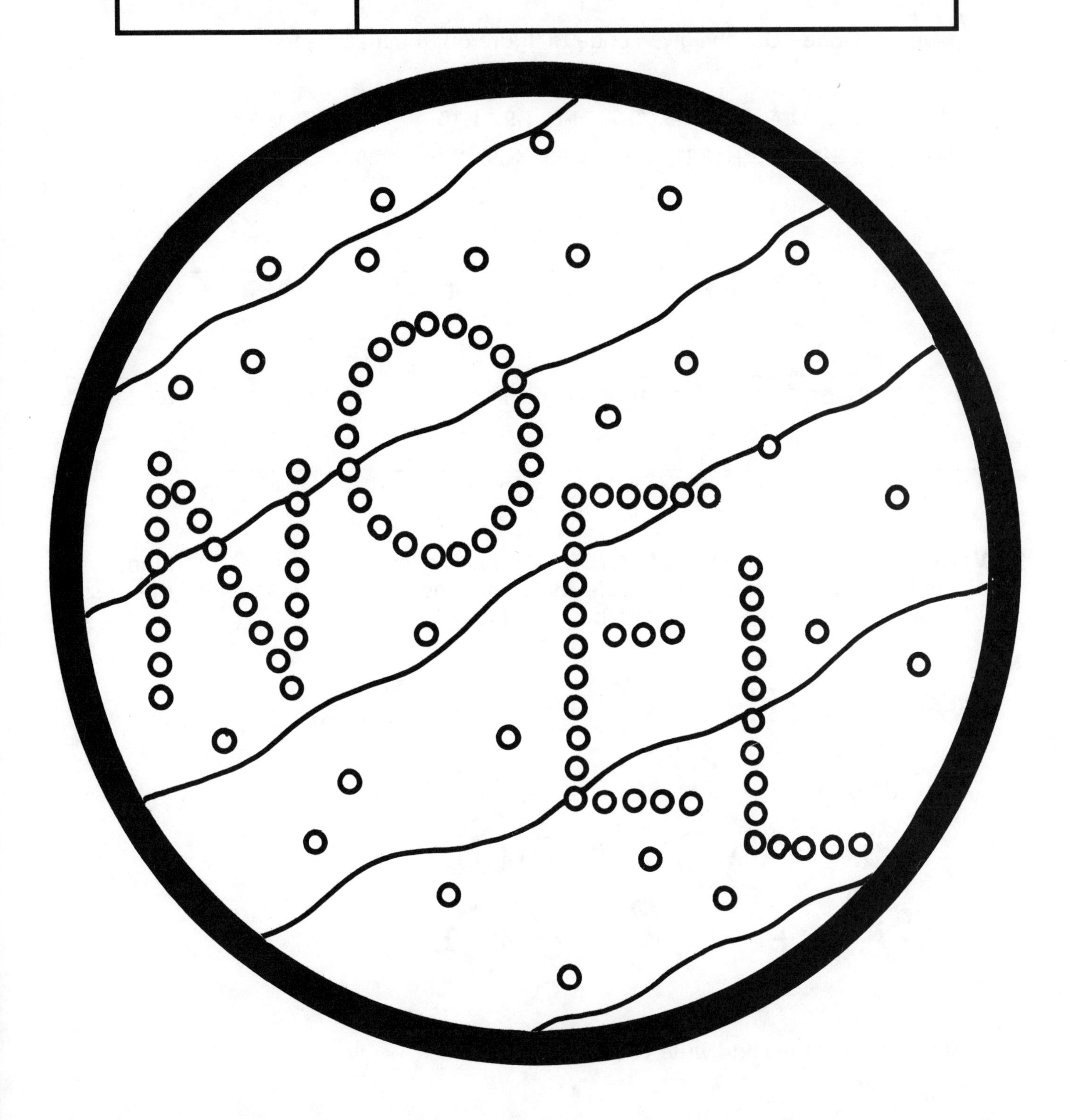

*N*oel, Noel,
Born is a king.
He came to save us.
Rejoice and sing.

*N*umber Code—Use the given code to figure out the message.

A-1, B-2, C-3, D-4, E-5, F-6, G-7, H-8, I-9, J-10, K-11, L-12, M-13, N-14, O-15, P-16, Q-17, R-18, S-19, T-20, U-21, V-22, W-23, X-24, Y-25, Z-26

_ _ _ _ _   _ _   _ _ _   _ _   _ _ _
7 12 15 18 25   20 15   7 15 4   9 14   20 8 5

_ _ _ _ _ _ _   _ _ _   _ _   _ _ _ _ _   _ _ _ _ _
8 9 7 8 5 19 20   1 14 4   15 14   5 1 18 20 8   16 5 1 3 5

_ _ _ _   _ _ _ _   _ _ _ _ _ _   _ _ _
7 15 15 4   23 9 12 12   20 15 23 1 18 4   13 5 14

*N*azareth Rebus—Start with *NAZARETH*. Add and subtract all the letters in the words indicated by the pictures. Unscramble the remaining letters to see where this puzzle leads you. Write your final answer in the given blanks.

Unscramble the letters and write your answer.

___ ___ ___ ___ ___ ___ ___ ___ ___

NAZARETH GAME

Directions: Have a race to see who can make the most words using the letters in the word *NAZARETH* within a given time period.

O	*O* is for the *Orient* From whence the wise men came. Melchior, Gaspar, and Balthasar Some say were these kings' names.

O is for the *Orient*
From whence the wise men came.
Melchior, Gaspar, and Balthasar
Some say were these kings' names.

*O*pposites—In each sentence, cross out the word which makes the sentence incorrect and replace it with a word of opposite meaning. Write the correct word in the blank after the sentence.

1. Mary visited her cousin, Elisabeth, who was going to have a child while she was very young. ______________

2. The inn was empty.______________

3. Mary wrapped Jesus in loose clothes and laid Him in a manger.______________

4. An angel appeared to shepherds who were watching their flocks by day.______________

5. The shepherds were unafraid when an angel appeared to them. ______________

6. The wise men led a star to the place where Jesus was born. ______________

7. Wise men from the west came to honor the Christ Child. ______________

8. King Herod was happy to hear of the birth of the newborn king. ______________

*O*rnaments—Collect several round paper or plastic lids, such as the kind used for yogurt and instant baby food. Punch a hole in each one and tie a piece of yarn through it to form a loop which can be used for hanging the ornament on a tree. Use a pencil to trace the outline of each lid on a used Christmas card. Cut out the circle from each used Christmas card. Glue the circles onto the lids. Hang the ornaments on a tree when the glue has dried.

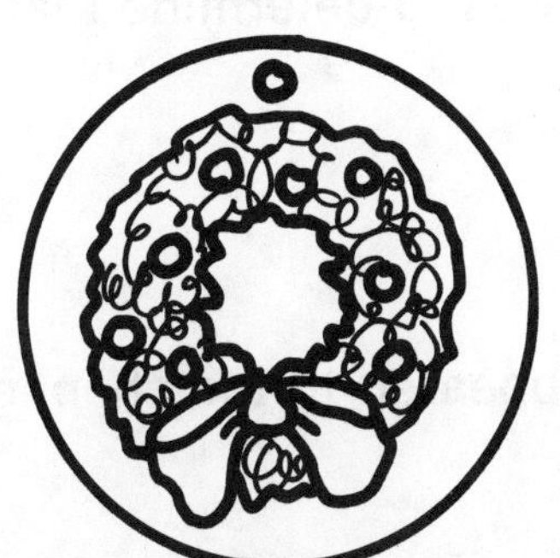

ONE, TWO, THREE TRIVIA

Directions: Divide the players into two teams. Alternate questions between the teams. The first player on Team One indicates whether trying for a one, two, or three point question. (The greater the points, the greater the difficulty.) If answered correctly, that number of points is scored for his/her team. If answered incorrectly, no points are scored. It is then the other team's turn. The first team to reach twenty-five points wins.

ONE-POINT QUESTIONS

1. On what date do most North Americans customarily celebrate Christ's birth?
2. Which angel appeared to Mary?
3. Where did Mary lay Jesus right after He was born?
4. Which king wished Jesus evil?
5. Who was the mother of Jesus?
6. Who was Mary's husband?
7. What did the wise men use to guide them to the baby Jesus?
8. Does the Bible tell us that Mary rode a donkey to Bethlehem?
9. What three gifts did the wise men bring?
10. Who were the Magi?

TWO-POINT QUESTIONS

1. Which two Gospels tell about Christ's birth?
2. What were the first two words the angel said to the shepherds?
3. What cousin did Mary visit while she was with child?
4. What name was given to Elisabeth's baby?
5. What are swaddling clothes?
6. Why did Joseph have to go to Bethlehem?
7. Which Gospel tells about the shepherds' visit to Jesus?
8. Which Gospel tells about the wise men's visit to Jesus?
9. To what country did the family flee?
10. Was Bethlehem in Galilee or Judea?

THREE-POINT QUESTIONS

1. What are the three names traditionally given the wise men?
2. Who was the governor of Syria when the taxing was first made?
3. Give two names for the city in which Christ was born.
4. What sign did the angel say could be used by the shepherds to determine that they had found the Savior?
5. What was the name of Elisabeth's husband?
6. What does Emmanuel mean?
7. On what day after His birth was Jesus given His name?
8. What are frankincense and myrrh?
9. What did the multitude of heavenly host say when they appeared to the shepherds?
10. What is a manger?

P	*Peace* on earth, goodwill toward men This joyous Christmas Day. Let harmony and love *prevail*, For this we humbly *pray*.

Peace on earth, goodwill toward men
This joyous Christmas Day.
Let harmony and love *prevail*,
For this we humbly *pray*.

Paper Punch Picture—Use a paper punch to punch out several dots from white or brightly colored scraps of construction paper. Use the dots to spell the word *peace* on a black sheet of construction paper. Be sure to use very tiny drops of glue. You can squeeze about ten or fifteen drops at a time and quickly cover them with the paper dots before the glue dries. Repeat this process until the entire word is spelled.

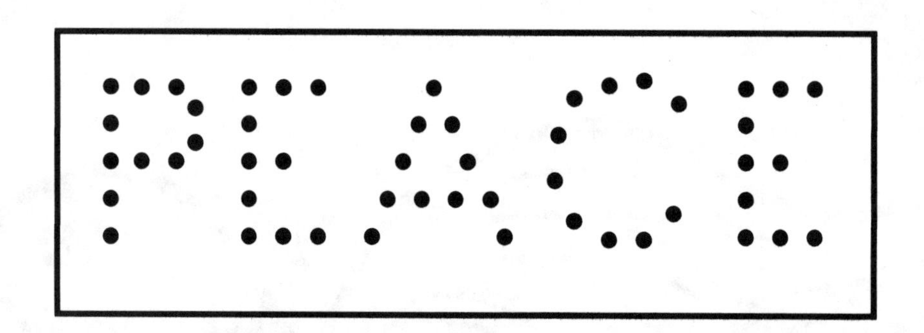

Puppet Play—Color and cut out the finger puppets below. Use them to put on a finger play about Christ's birth.

PEACE PUZZLE RACE

Directions: Use your Bible to look up the verses listed on the puzzle pieces. Then cover the circle sections with the matching pieces. You can also use this puzzle for a race. The first player to cover the circle correctly is the winner.

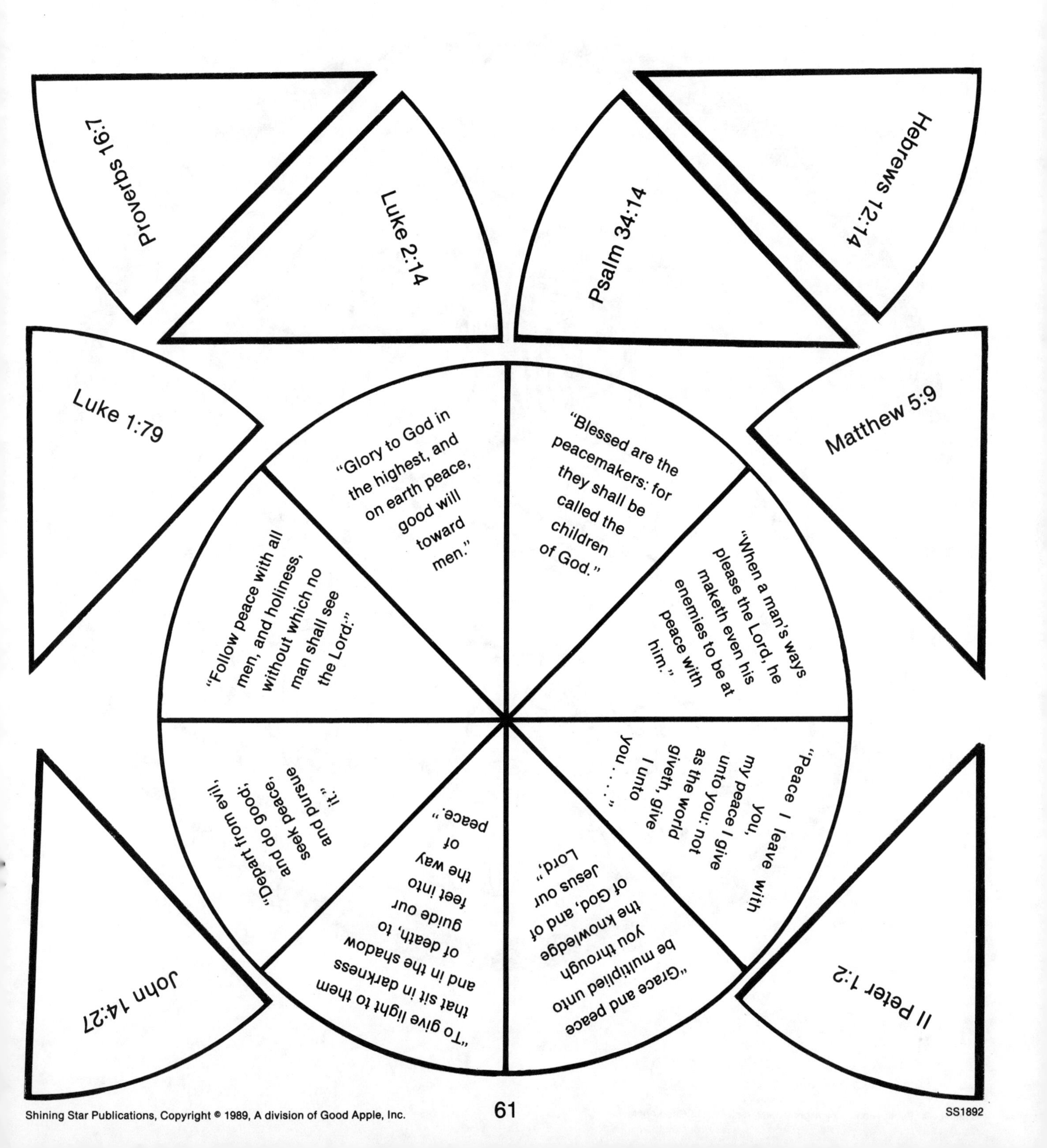

Q is for the *quietude*
That surrounds the manger scene,
The holy Child at its center
So peaceful and serene.

Q is for the *quietude*
That surrounds the manger scene,
The holy Child at its center
So peaceful and serene.

*Q*uiz Questions—Write the answer to each question on the given blanks. All questions refer to the Nativity story.

1. Who ordered that a census be taken?________________
2. Who brought gifts of gold, frankincense, and myrrh?________________
3. Who was warned in a dream to flee with his family to Egypt?________________
4. Who wanted to harm Christ, the newborn King?________________
5. Who told Mary she would bear a son?________________
6. Who did the angel appear to in the fields?________________
7. Who was born to save us?________________
8. Who was born to Mary's cousin, Elisabeth?________________

*Q*uestion Game—Use the question mark below as a gameboard. Use small items for game markers. Place each person's (or team's) game marker on the question mark dot at the start of the game. You will need a leader to ask questions like the ones in the quiz above. All questions must pertain to the Nativity story. Take turns answering the leader's questions. When a question is answered correctly, the person or team may advance the marker one space. When a question has been answered incorrectly, the marker remains on the same space. In either case, it is the next person's (or team's) turn. The person or team to reach the other end of the question mark first is the winner.

QUESTIONS ARE ANSWERS

Directions: You will need a leader and two to four other people to play this game. Each player chooses a marker and places it on START. The leader then gives an answer. (For example, "She conceived a son in her old age.") The first person to give the correct question to go with the answer may move ahead one space. (For example, "Who was Elisabeth?") The first player to reach FINISH is the winner. The leader may need to use some of the items more than once if all the items have been used before someone wins. All the questions and answers are about the material in the first two chapters of Matthew and Luke.

To play this game in class, draw a large question mark on the chalkboard. Divide the players into teams and assign each team a number. Teams can keep track of their progress by writing their team numbers and erasing them with each move. Play the rest of the game as indicated in the directions above.

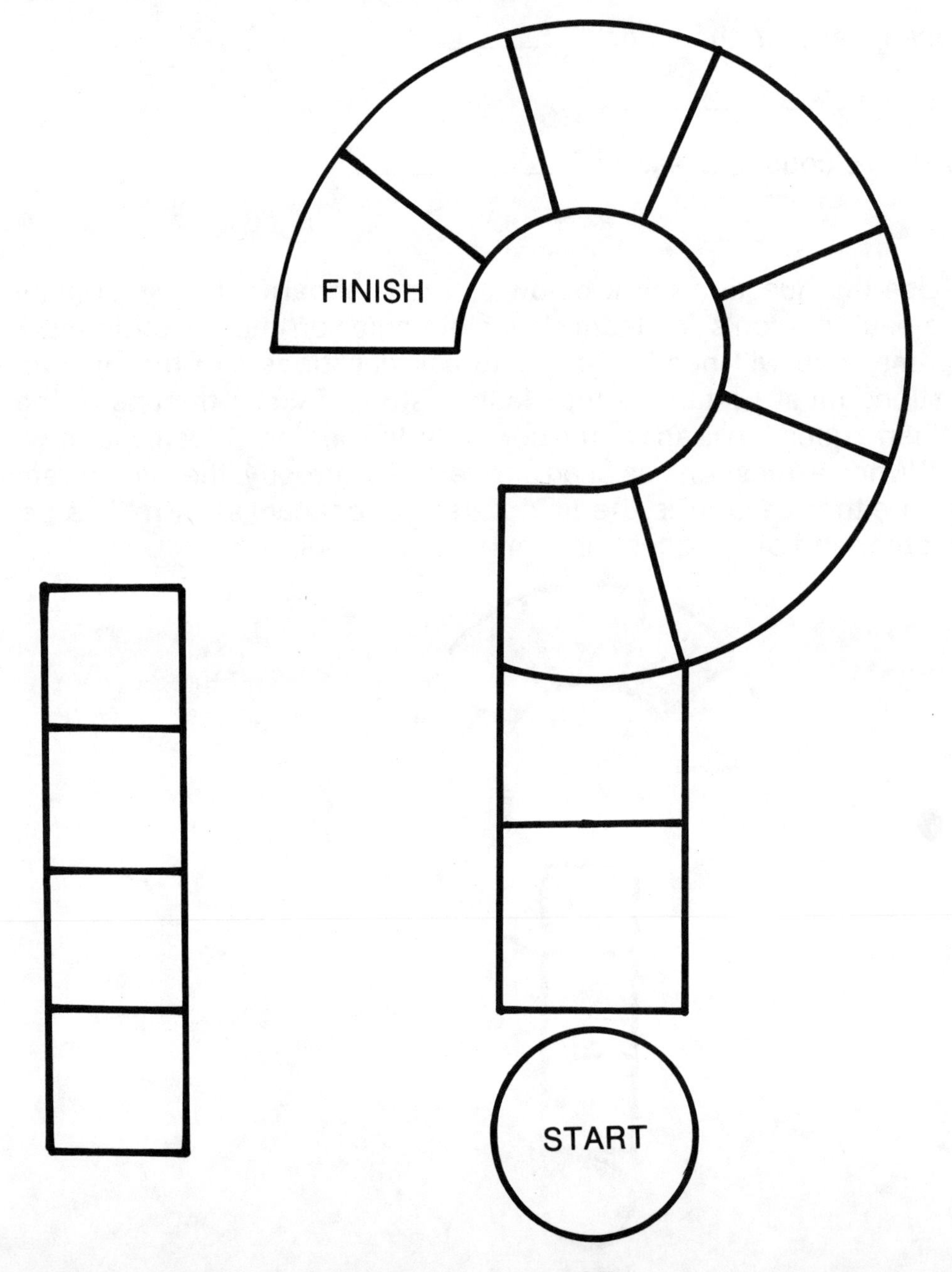

LEADER'S ANSWERS AND QUESTIONS FOR "QUESTIONS ARE ANSWERS"

1. She conceived a son in her old age.
   Who was Elisabeth?
2. A trough for feeding animals
   What is a manger?
3. She was the mother of Jesus.
   Who was Mary?
4. A building in which travelers stay
   What is an inn?
5. He was speechless while his wife was with child, but was able to speak at the naming of his son.
   Who was Zacharias?
6. He was sent from God to deliver a message to a virgin.
   Who was the angel Gabriel?
7. The city where Jesus was born
   What is Bethlehem?
8. A precious metal given as a gift to the baby Jesus
   What is gold?
9. This son of Elisabeth preached the baptism of repentance for the remission of sins.
   Who was John?
10. The place where Mary and Joseph went to worship God
    What is a temple?
11. An amount paid by individuals to a government
    What is a tax?
12. He decreed that all the world should be taxed.
    Who was Caesar Augustus?
13. An object that rose in the east at the birth of Christ
    What is a star?
14. He was espoused to Mary.
    Who was Joseph?
15. It was revealed to him that he would not die before he saw the Christ.
    Who was Simeon?
16. Tight strips of cloth wrapped around an infant
    What are swaddling clothes?
17. Men from the east who brought Jesus gifts
    Who were the wise men (or Magi or kings)?
18. This king did not want Jesus to be king.
    Who was Herod?
19. The place to which the holy family fled
    What is Egypt?
20. They were watching their flocks when an angel appeared.
    Who were the shepherds?

R	*Radiant* was the star that *rose* And shone upon the earth; The beacon guided visitors To the place of Jesus' birth.

*R*adiant was the star that *rose*
And shone upon the earth;
The beacon guided visitors
To the place of Jesus' birth.

*R*iddle Rhymes—Write the answer to each riddle.

1. The three wise men used my light
   To guide them safely through the night. ____________________

2. Frankincense and myrrh were brought to the newborn king.
   What other gift did the wise men bring? ____________________

3. I often carry a heavy sack.
   It is said that Mary rode upon my back. ____________________

4. I told shepherds in the night
   Where they could find a wondrous sight. ____________________

5. This is where animals are usually fed,
   But Jesus used me as a bed. ____________________

*R*ebus Fun—Carefully add and subtract letters to spell the answer to each rebus.

RHYME GAME

Directions: This game is for two players. First, paste the cards onto cardboard and cut them out. Deal 5 cards to each player. Place the remaining 10 cards face down in a pile. The first player looks at the cards in his/her hand. After choosing a card, the player asks for a card that rhymes with it. For example, if deciding to use the card marked *EARTH*, the player would say the following to the other player: "Do you have a card that rhymes with *EARTH*?" If the other player has such a card, it must be given to the first player. If the other player does not have a rhyming card, he/she points to the pile and says, "Pick a card from there. It might make a rhyming pair." Every time a card matches, either from the other player or from the pile, the player gets another turn. Players alternate asking for cards. The winner is the first person to get rid of all his/her cards.

EARTH	BIRTH	NIGHT	LIGHT
BOY	JOY	SIN	INN
NEWS	JEWS	STAR	FAR
KING	BRING	CHILD	MILD
MANGER	DANGER	GOLD	TOLD

S	*Some shepherds* were watching their *sheep* When an angel appeared and said That a *Savior* wrapped in *swaddling* clothes Could be found in a manger bed.

Some shepherds were watching their *sheep*
When an angel appeared and said
That a *Savior* wrapped in *swaddling* clothes
Could be found in a manger bed.

Scrambled Sentences—Rearrange each group of words to form a sentence that pertains to the Bible.

1. to angel appeared The Mary Gabriel

 ____

2. visited cousin Mary Elisabeth her

 ____

3. wrapped swaddling Mary clothes Jesus in

 ____

4. in lying found a The manger shepherds Jesus

 ____

5. to the child Herod soldiers search sent for

 ____

Sheep Search—Choose someone to hide several cotton ball "sheep." The rest of the players should act like good shepherds and find the sheep. The one finding the most may hide them next.

Sticker Stories—Write a short story about the birth of Christ. Leave out some words and use religious stickers to represent the words.

SKETCHING FROM SCRIPTURES

Directions: On the dark lines, cut out the words found below. Divide into two teams. The first player on Team One picks one of the slips of paper from a hat. The player then must draw pictures on the chalkboard or on a large piece of paper without speaking. The other players on that team must try to guess what Nativity word is being sketched. If they can do so in under one minute (the time can be increased or decreased depending on the ability of the group), the team scores a point. If not, no point is scored. In either case, it is the next team's turn to draw and guess. The winning team is the one having the most points after all the slips have been used. Try a challenge game using Bible phrases such as "good will toward men."

JESUS	**MARY**
BETHLEHEM	**JOSEPH**
ANGEL	**INN**
MANGER	**STAR**
KING HEROD	**EARTH**
GOLD	**SHEPHERDS**
EARTH	**WISE MEN**
HANDMAID	**EAST**
FRANKINCENSE	**FLEE**
HOUSE	**DREAM**

T	*To terrified* and *trembling* shepherds The angel messenger said, "Fear not." *Tidings* of great joy Is what the angel brought.

To terrified and *trembling* shepherds
The angel messenger said, "Fear not."
Tidings of great joy
Is what the angel brought.

Tissue Paper Project—On a sheet of construction paper, draw a sheep, star, shepherd, king's crown, or other Christmas symbol. Loosely roll several one-inch squares of brightly colored tissue paper into small balls. Glue the tissue paper balls onto your drawing. Try to use several bright colors on your project.

Tiding Tree—Obtain several brightly colored lids of the same size. Use lids with white centers or paste white circles inside the lids. Glue them onto a piece of green poster board to form a tree shaped as indicated in the illustration below. Use bright colors to write a Christmas greeting on each. Perhaps you would like to make it an international tree by writing Christmas greetings in several languages.

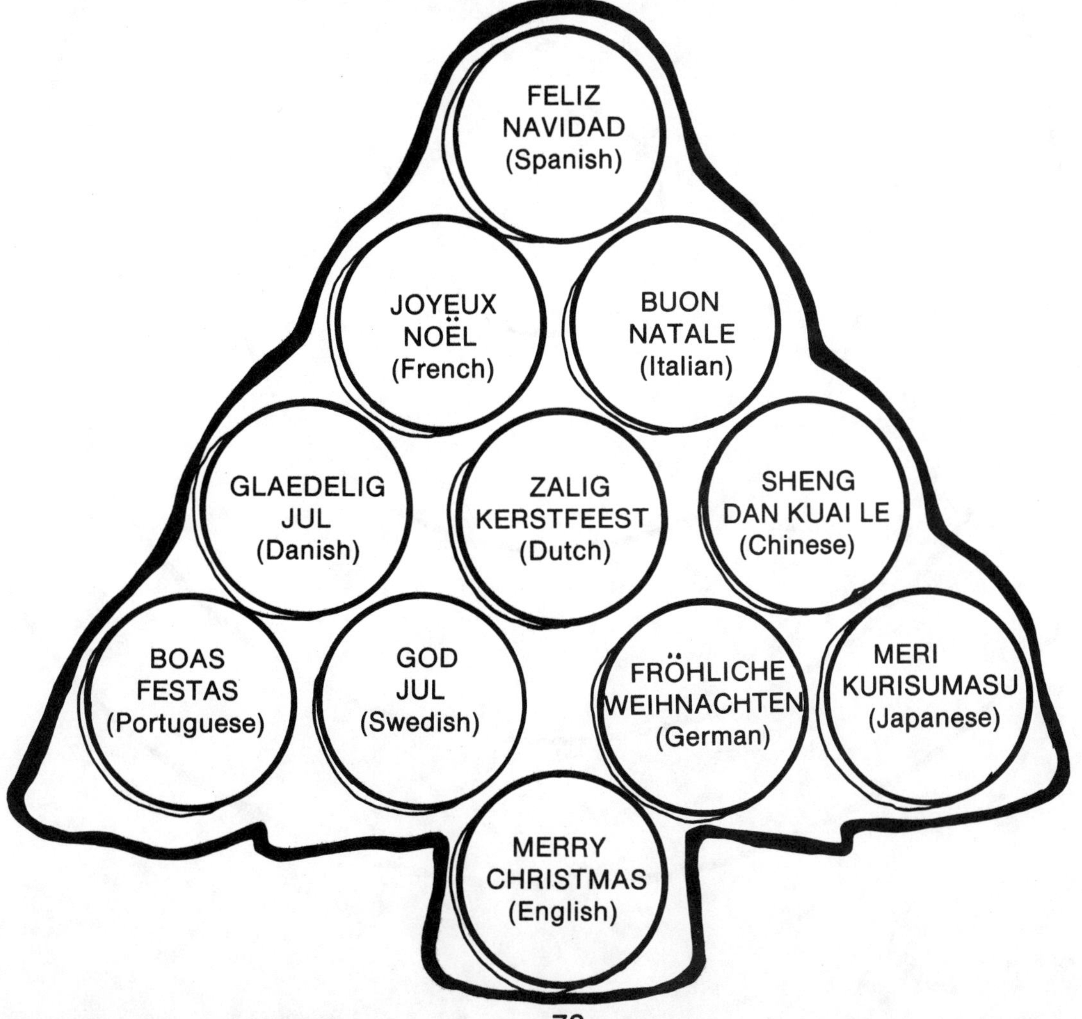

TIDINGS TOSS

Directions: Take turns tossing a coin at the target. A player whose coin lands mostly in the space marked with a *J* scores two points. One whose coin lands mostly in the space marked with an *O* scores five points. One whose coin lands mostly in the space marked *Y* scores ten points. After five rounds, the player with the most points wins. If the game is played by teams, let each player toss one coin. Then add up the scores for each team.

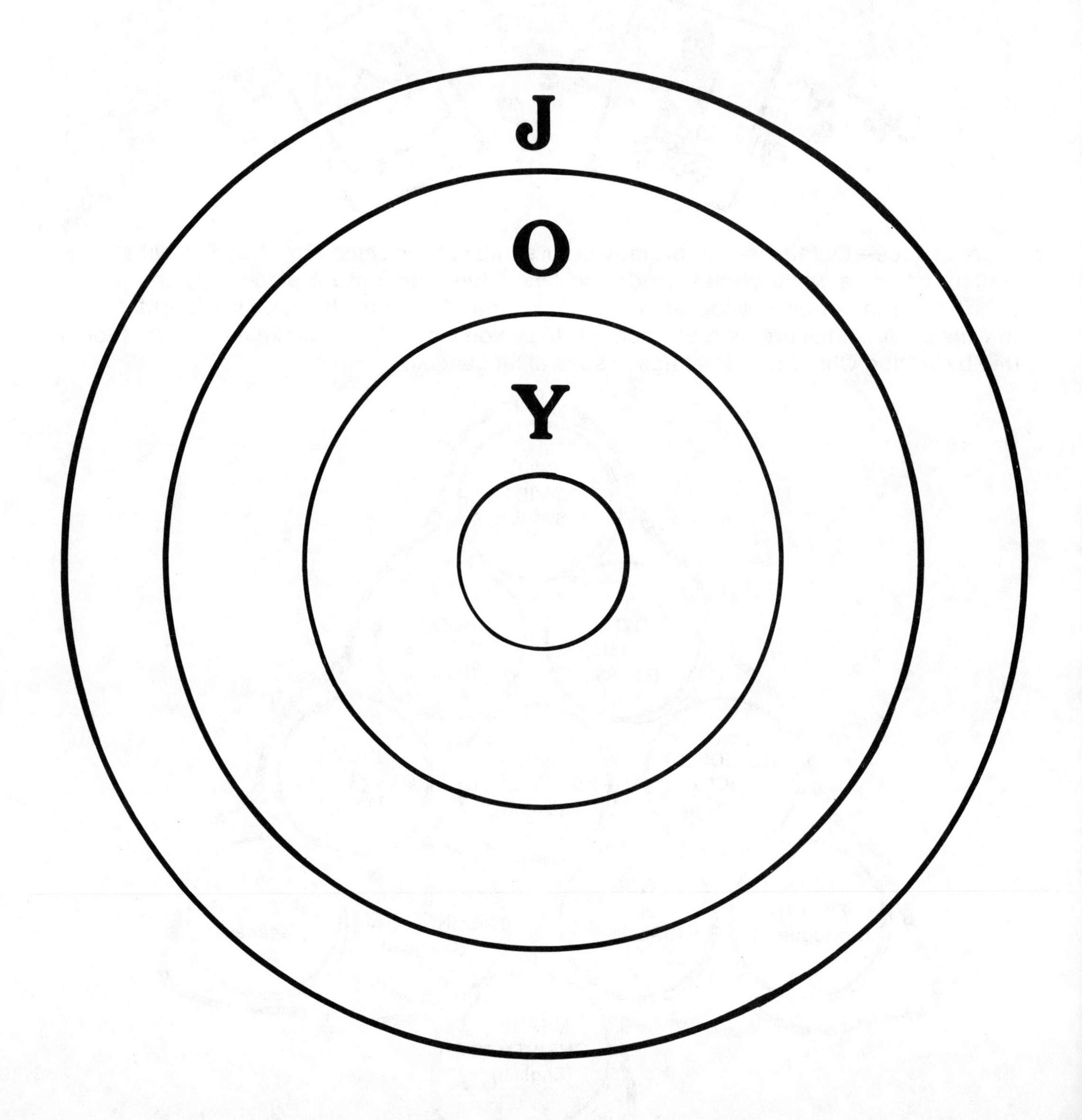

U

"*Unto* you a child is born,"
The angel messenger said.
The shepherds made the message known
And so the news was spread.

"Unto you a child is born,"
The angel messenger said.
The shepherds made the message known
And so the news was spread.

Unscrambling Activity—Rearrange the letters to spell words about the Christmas story.

1. YAH	____________	8. MERANG	____________
2. TINDIGS	____________	9. HEEPS	____________
3. POSEHJ	____________	10. METHEELBH	____________
4. BRAGLIE	____________	11. HISTRC	____________
5. GAIM	____________	12. RINKPENEE	____________
6. MARED	____________	13. RODHE	____________
7. CARSEA	____________	14. SUNCES	____________

Underlining Activity—Underline the word which best finishes each sentence about the Christmas story.

1. Unto you a child is	kind	little	born
2. Glory to God in the	heavens	highest	church
3. I bring you good news of great	joy	happenings	comfort
4. I am the handmaid of the	servant	Lord	king
5. Blessed is the fruit of your	basket	tree	womb
6. Nothing will be impossible for	you	God	us
7. Where is the newborn King of the	town	world	Jews

UNSCRAMBLE A VERSE

Directions: Let children unscramble the given pieces to form Luke 2:11. A Christmas prize may be awarded to the first child who can do so. For fun, have children write verses from the Nativity story on slips of paper. Then have them cut the paper apart between the words. Have them put the pieces for each verse in a separate envelope. Let them exchange envelopes with one another to unscramble the verses.

CHRIST	YOU
THE	UNTO
SAVIOUR,	IS
DAVID	DAY
LORD.	THIS
WHICH	BORN
CITY	THE
FOR	IN
IS	OF
A	

V

V is for the *virgin* Mary,
So holy and so pure.
She is the mother of Jesus
And so we honor her.

SS1892

V is for the *virgin* Mary,
So holy and so pure.
She is the mother of Jesus
And so we honor her.

*V*owel Activity—Place vowels in the blanks to spell titles with which we honor Mary's son, Jesus.

C H R _ S T

L _ G H T   _ F   T H _   W _ R L D

M _ S S _ _ H

G _ _ D   S H _ P H _ R D

K _ N G   _ F   K _ N G S

L _ M B   _ F   G _ D

R _ D _ _ M _ R

S _ V _ _ _ R

P R _ N C _   _ F   L _ F _

P R _ N C _   O _   P _ _ C E

_ L P H _   _ N D   _ M _ G _

B R _ G H T   _ N D   M _ R N _ N G   S T _ R

*V*isiting—Visit a nursing home, hospital, shelter, or orphanage. Distribute Christmas cards or sing songs for all those there. Collect items to donate to the center you are visiting.

*V*isualization—Visualize the scene in the manger, at Herod's palace, during the Annunciation, or during the flight to Egypt. Draw your view of the scene on a separate sheet of paper.

VERSE VOYAGE

Directions: Try to spell out a verse by traveling through this maze of letters. Move vertically or horizontally from one letter to the next. You must travel in a path which hits all the letters once and only once. You might want to have a race against others. If you haven't solved the maze after ten minutes, you may want to look in the first chapter of Luke for hints.

N	G	M	E	E	S	
O	W	O	N	L	S	
M	A	U	A	B	E	
B	L	O	N	D	D	
START	E	H	T	S	I	
S	S	R	T	T	H	
E	D	A	I	U	E	
T	F	O	T	R	F	
H	Y	W	O	M	B	FINISH

W	*W* is for the *wondrous* star Which led the *wise men* through Herod's land. These *worshippers* returned another *way* When *warned* of his evil plan.

W is for the *wondrous* star
Which led the *wise men* through Herod's land.
These *worshippers* returned another *way*
When *warned* of his evil plan.

*W*reath—On heavy paper, draw a small circle inside a larger circle. Cut out to form a wreath. Cut out and decorate three paper crowns and some stars. Glue them to the wreath. Add a bow. The finished product will look something like the drawing shown.

*W*ord Search—You will find seventeen words hidden inside the crown if you search across, backwards, up, down and diagonally.

FRANKINCENSE
ASTROLOGERS
BALTHASAR
BETHLEHEM
THREE

WISE MEN
HOMAGE
GASPAR
MELCHIOR

MYRRH
GIFTS
HEROD
KINGS

MAGI
EAST
STAR
GOLD

D									E	M									E
G	M							T	A	P	A							F	S
S	A	A					O	D	S	B	U	G					B	R	N
W	G	S	I			W	I	S	E	M	E	N	I			A	E	M	E
I	A	M	P	G	I	F	S	W	A	R	H	T	H	R	E	G	T	E	C
S	S	E	G	A	S	P	R	I	S	E	E	R	H	T	O	A	H	L	N
E	T	L	R	H	R	R	Y	M	T	N	R	H	C	L	E	M	L	C	I
M	R	C	B	E	T	H	L	E	H	E	D	D	O	R	E	H	E	H	K
N	A	H	O	M	A	G	E	N	O	M	Y	R	H	H	Y	H	H	O	N
S	K	I	N	G	S	O	M	B	A	L	T	H	A	S	A	R	E	R	A
A	G	O	L	E	D	L	R	G	F	S	A	G	I	F	T	S	T	M	R
T	F	R	A	T	S	D	O	T	A	K	I	N	S	T	H	R	E	S	F

WHAT'S THE WORD?

Directions: You will need two teams of two players each for this game. You will also need a fifth player to act as leader. Each team needs a clue giver and a clue guesser for round one. The leader picks a word and shows it to the clue giver from each team. Team One's clue giver tries to get his/her partner to guess what the word is by giving a one-word clue. The clue giver has fifteen seconds to think of a clue and the clue guesser has fifteen seconds to make a guess. The leader acts as the timer. If Team One's clue guesser does not get the answer correct, it is Team Two's turn to give a clue and make a guess. If the guess is incorrect, it is Team One's turn to give another clue. When a team member guesses correctly, a point is scored for that team. Whenever a team scores a point, they get to give the first clue of the next round. The clue givers and guessers on both teams switch jobs for the next round. (If a word has not been guessed after six total clues, the word is eliminated from the game. The same players continue to act as clue givers and the same team goes first.) After eight words have been used, the team scoring the most points wins. Enough words have been provided for three games. (The previous leader can then play and someone else can act as leader.)

FRANKINCENSE	MOTHER	DREAM
GOVERNOR	JOY	PEACE
SOUL	HOLY	HEART
WOMEN	WIFE	MONTH
WORSHIP	FLEE	DESTROY
PROPHET	AFRAID	CLOTHES
WORLD	CITY	FLOCK
FIELD	DECREE	TREASURES

X-mas is Christmas
With the word "Christ" left out,
But those who call it this
Are missing what Christmas is about.

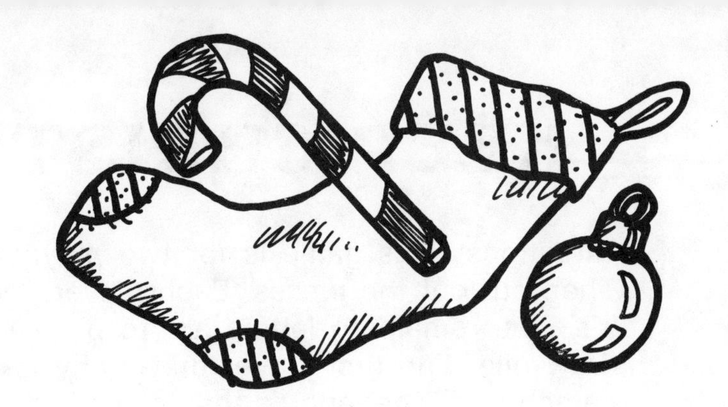

X-mas is Christmas
With the word "Christ" left out,
But those who call it this
Are missing what Christmas is about.

X Out Rhymes—Use an *X* to cross out the word which doesn't rhyme in each row.

1. HER	HERE	MYRRH	10. GOLD	COLD	CALLED
2. SHEEP	SLEEP	SHAPE	11. HAY	HAIL	LAY
3. STAY	STABLE	FABLE	12. KIND	KING	BRING
4. STAR	FAR	STARE	13. TALK	FLOCK	TAKE
5. FEAR	FAR	NEAR	14. NEWS	NOSE	CHOOSE
6. LATE	NIGHT	LIGHT	15. BORN	MORN	BARN
7. COMB	COME	FROM	16. CHILD	CHILL	MILD
8. ANGER	MANGER	DANGER	17. GOOD	SHOULD	GOD
9. FALL	FLEE	FREE	18. SAME	SEEM	DREAM

X Out Message— Cross out all the letters which appear twelve times. Write the remaining letters in order in the blanks below to spell out a message.

FKEARVMNOMTVFOMRBEMHVOLDVIBRMIKNGKYOKUGOMOVDTVIKDIMN
GKSVOKFGKREMAVTJOMYWVHKICHSHMAKLVLBKEVTOMKALLPEMOPLVE

"..._ _ _ _ _   _ _ _: _ _ _,   _ _ _ _ _ _ _ _,   _

_ _ _ _ _ _   _ _ _   _ _ _ _ _   _ _ _ _ _ _ _ _ _   _ _

_ _ _ _ _ _   _ _ _,   _ _ _ _ _ _   _ _ _ _ _ _   _ _   _ _

_ _ _   _ _ _ _ _ _ _ _." Luke 2:10

KEEP CHRIST IN CHRISTMAS

Directions: This game is for two players. Glue this page onto a sheet of cardboard. Then cut out the pieces. Each player needs one gameboard marked *Christmas* and 9 *X*'s. The remaining letters are to be placed face down between the two players in a draw pile. The first player draws any letter, using an *X* to mark off that letter on the gameboard. The letter is then placed onto a discard pile. The next player draws a letter and does the same thing. The players take turns drawing letters and covering their gameboards with *X*'s. If a player can't use a letter, it is returned to the draw pile and mixed up with the remaining letters. The first person who covers the first six letters (C-H-R-I-S-T) is the loser, because the object of the game to is try to keep Christ in Christmas.

GAMEBOARDS

C	H	R	I	S	T	M	A	S
C	H	R	I	S	T	M	A	S

LETTERS FOR DRAW PILE

C	H	R	I	S	T	M	A	S
C	H	R	I	S	T	M	A	S

X'S FOR EACH PLAYER

X	X	X	X	X	X	X	X	X
X	X	X	X	X	X	X	X	X

Y	*Yuletide* messages come to *you* At Christmastime each *year* To fill your heart with love and joy, Gladness and good cheer.

*Y*uletide messages come to *you*
At Christmastime each *year*
To fill your heart with love and joy,
Gladness and good cheer.

*Y*arn Pictures—Sketch a religious Christmas picture. Fill in your sketch by gluing small pieces of yarn to it. For example, yellow yarn can be used for hay or to fill in a star. Other colors can be used for other parts of your picture.

*Y*uletide Messages—
These season's greetings come to you to brighten up your day,
Tucked inside an envelope in a very special way.
Find and circle Christmas words in the puzzle given below.
Then spread these season's messages to everyone you know.

GLORY TO GOD
FEAR NOT
CHRIST THE LORD
FRANKINCENSE
WISE MEN
PEACE

BETHLEHEM
GREAT JOY
SAVIOUR
GOLD
SHEPHERDS

GOOD WILL
GOOD TIDINGS
REJOICE
MYRRH
ANGELS

G G B R E J O I C E D W I S E C M
L R L W I S E M E N A E E C E H A
O Y G O O D W I L L N L A H N A N
B F E A R N O T E S G E R P S R G
E M B G L Y P E A C P S D E H D E
T Y E M O G T T O S A V I O U R L
H R T E R O G O O D T I D I N G S
L R H H Y D O D G R E A T J O Y C
E H L E T X L G O O M A N B O E N
H R E J O I D C E D D G O D L K I
E F R A N K I N C E N S E F R A N
M C H R I S T T H E L O R D R N C
G R E A T J S H E P H E R D S I E

YULETIDE MESSAGES

Directions: Distribute a used Christmas card to each child. Call out five of the words given below or write them on the board. The child who can find the most words on his/her card wins. Play several rounds. Then redistribute the cards and play several more rounds.

GOD	HOLY	BORN	ANGEL	CHEER
JOY	LOVE	PEACE	HEART	HOLIDAY
BLESS	CHRISTMAS	JESUS	BABY	WORLD
MERRY	FRIEND	INFANT	STAR	TIDINGS
HAPPY	NOEL	WISH	GREETINGS	CHILD

YEAR	GIFTS	SPIRIT	SON	ALWAYS
GLORY	REJOICE	SAVIOR	BRING	WONDER
GOODWILL	DAY	SEASON	HOPE	MANGER
BRIGHT	BEAUTIFUL	INFANT	CHRIST	LORD
LITTLE	SHEPHERDS	WARMTH	MEN	PRAISE

Z	*Zacharias* and Elisabeth's son, John, Was born in ancient days. He went before the Lord To help prepare His ways.

*Z*acharias and Elisabeth's son, John,
Was born in ancient days.
He went before the Lord
To help prepare His ways.

*Z*igzag Name Puzzles—Print the following names on narrow strips of oak tag or poster board. Then cut different zigzags to separate the names into two parts. Mix up all the pieces and try to put the names back together.

MARY	JOSEPH	JESUS	GABRIEL	ELISABETH
JOHN	HEROD	EMMANUEL	MELCHIOR	ZACHARIAS
BALTHASAR	GASPAR	CAESAR		

*Z*ippered Pouch Activities—Follow the directions given.

1. Store twenty-five pieces of straw or twenty-five yellow pipe cleaners in a zippered pouch. Starting on December 1, add one piece of straw or one pipe cleaner to a manger box each day. On the 25th, add the last piece and a figure of the baby Jesus.
2. Write twenty-five good deeds on separate slips of paper. Store them in a zippered pouch. Starting on December 1, randomly choose one slip of paper and do the good deed written on it that day. Continue choosing a deed every day until Christmas.
3. Have an adult write twenty-five questions about Christ's birth on separate slips of paper. Store them in a zippered pouch along with twenty-five Christmas stickers. Starting on December 1, randomly choose one question to answer. If answered correctly, you may pick a sticker. Let someone else have a turn the next day. Take turns until Christmas. If a question is answered incorrectly, it goes back into the zippered pouch and may be randomly chosen on another day. On Christmas Day, take turns trying to get the remaining answers correct (if any) until all the stickers are gone.

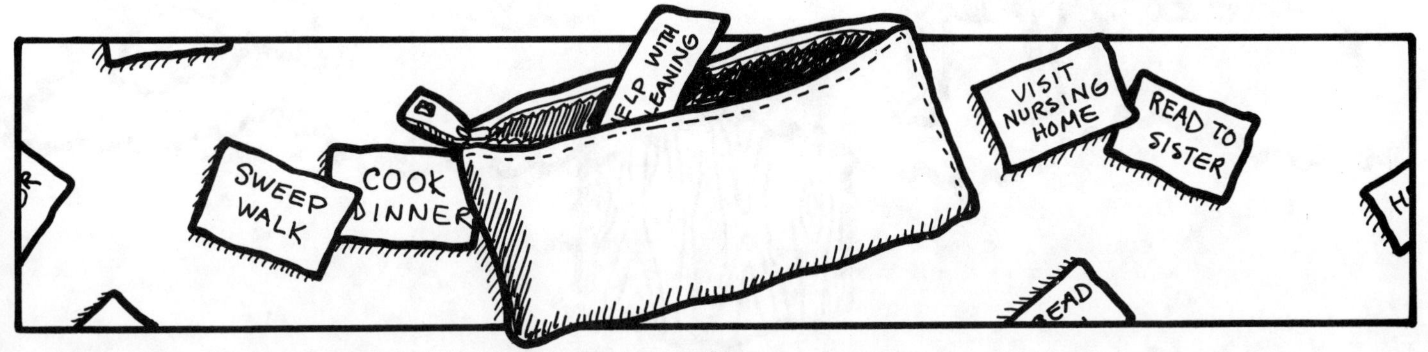

A-Z MEMORY GAME

Directions: The object of this game is to try to remember Christmas words from *A*-*Z*. The first player starts by saying: "Christmas is for ______________." (The player fills in the blank with a word beginning with *A*. The next player repeats the *A* word and adds on a *B* word. The third player says "Christmas is for ______________, ______________, and ______________." (The player repeats the previous *A* and *B* words and adds on a *C* word.) If a player cannot remember all the words or cannot think of a word, he/she is out of the game. All words must somehow be related to Christmas. All the players still left when the game gets to the letter *Z* are winners. If the game does not progress that far, the last person out wins.

ANSWER KEY

Arranging Sentences page 14
1. 3; 2. 2; 3. 4; 4. 1; 5. 6; 6. 5

Anagrams page 14
1. Mary; 2. field; 3. star; 4. angel; 5. east

ABC Game page 15
1. Lord; 2. dream; 3. myrrh; 4. highest; 5. tidings; 6. shepherds; 7. son; 8. Nazareth; 9. Herod; 10. David

Bethlehem Blanks page 17
b-irthday, e-arth, t-hree, h-oly, l-ight, E-gypt, H-erod, e-ast, M-agi

Crossword Puzzle page 20
across: 1. city 3. clothes 4. Caesar
down: 1. Child 2. census

Census page 20
Twenty people are in the puzzle.

Elimination Game page 27
1. T; 2. T; 3. F; 4. F; 5. F (The number of wise men is not mentioned.); 6. T; 7. F; 8.T; 9. F; 10. F; 11. F; 12. F; 13. T; 14. F; 15. F; 16. T; 17. F; 18. T; 19. T; 20. F

Fill-Ins page 29
1. gift; 2. king; 3. Magi; 4. bring; 5. gold

Go Search for Good News page 33
1. women; 2. thee (you); 3. Highest; 4. Jacob; 5. end; 6. impossible; 7. joy; 8. David; 9. peace; 10. men

Hidden Pictures page 35

Jumbled Words page 41
1. Christ; 2. Savior; 3. Redeemer; 4. Lord; 5. Emmanuel; 6. King; 7. Infant; 8. Messiah; 9. Son; 10. Light

Hidden Words page 41

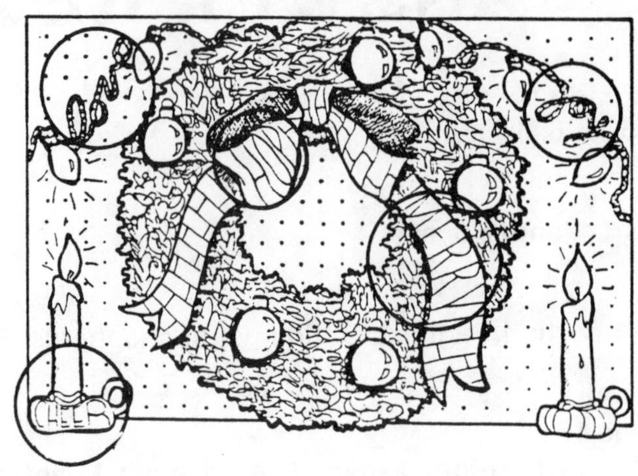

Jesus, Mary, and Joseph Game page 42
1. Jesus; 2. Jesus; 3. Mary; 4. Mary; 5. Joseph; 6. Mary; 7. Jesus; 8. Mary; 9. Jesus; 10. Jesus; 11. Mary; 12. Mary; 13. Jesus; 14. Joseph; 15. Mary

Kingly Knowledge page 45
1. Magi, astrologers, wise men; 2. Melchior, Balthasar, Gaspar; 3. frankincense, myrrh, gold

Kings Three page 45
frankincense, Bethlehem, Augustus, Nazareth, Galilee, Gabriel, Balthasar, Melchior, Syria, multitude

King's Race page 46
1. Rehoboam; 2. Solomon; 3. Asa; 4. Wise Man #1; 5. Wise Man #2; 6. Wise Man #3; 7. Ahab; 8. Herod; 9. Hezekiah

Life of Jesus Link-Ups page 49
1. Bethlehem; 2. Mary; 3. Herod; 4. wise men; 5. Egypt; 6. temple; 7. Nazareth; 8. John; 9. devil; 10. disciples; 11. Cana; 12. temple; 13. fish; 14. Jerusalem; 15. parables; 16. passover; 17. Judas; 18. Pilate; 19. thorns; 20. cross

Maze page 51

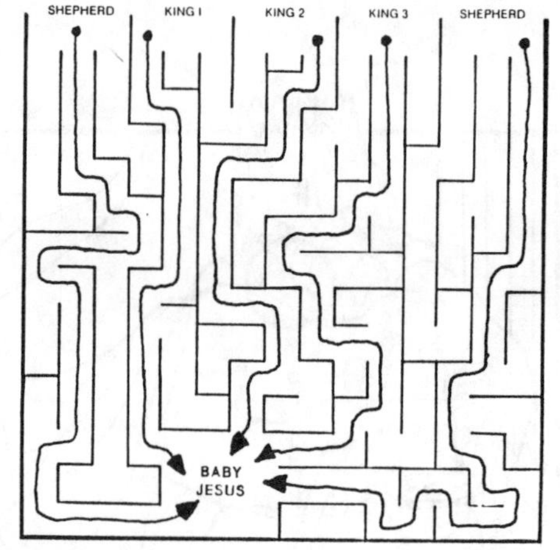

Mary, the Mother of Jesus page 52
(Answers will vary. One possibility is given.)
Books: Micah, Obadiah, Timothy, Hosea, Ezekiel, Revelation; Places: Moab, Ophir, Trye, Hepher, Ephraim, Ramoth-gilead; People: Manasses, Ozias, Thomas, Herod, Esrom, Roboam

Number Code page 54
Glory to God in the highest and on earth peace, good will toward men.

Nazareth Rebus page 54

Nazareth Game page 55
(These are just some samples. Any word formed by using the given letters are acceptable.) an, at, are, art, ant, hat, tan, hare, rent, than, then, ear, tear, rat, tar, near, neat, heat, hear, heart, earth

Opposites page 57
1. young-old; 2. empty-full; 3. loose-swaddling or tight; 4. day-night; 5. unafraid-afraid; 6. led-followed; 7. west-east; 8. happy-unhappy

One, Two, Three Trivia page 58
One-point questions: 1. December 25th; 2. Gabriel; 3. manger; 4. Herod; 5. Mary; 6. Joseph; 7. a star; 8. no; 9. gold, frankincense, and myrrh; 10. the wise men or kings

Two-point questions: 1. Matthew and Luke; 2. Fear not; 3. Elisabeth; 4. John; 5. strips of cloth wrapped tightly around a baby; 6. to be taxed; 7. Luke; 8. Matthew; 9. Egypt; 10. Judea

Three-point questions: 1. Melchior, Gaspar, and Balthasar; 2. Cyrenius; 3. Bethlehem and the city of David; 4."... Ye shall find the babe wrapped in swaddling clothes, lying in a manger."; 5. Zacharias; 6. God with us; 7. the eighth; 8. gum resins used as incense and perfume; 9. "Glory to God in the highest, and on earth peace, good will toward men."; 10. a box or trough to hold feed for animals

Peace Puzzle Race page 61
John 14:27-"Peace I . . . ,"; Matthew 5:9-"Blessed are . . . ,"; Luke 2:14-"Glory to God . . . ,"; Psalm 34:14-"Depart from evil . . . ,"; Luke 1:79-"To give light . . . ,"; II Peter 1:2-"Grace and peace . . . ,"; Hebrews 12:14-"Follow . . . ,"; Proverbs 16:7-"When a man's ways . . . ."

Quiz Questions page 63
1. Caesar Augustus; 2. the wise men; 3. Joseph; 4. Herod; 5. the angel Gabriel; 6. the shepherds; 7. Jesus; 8. John

Riddle Rhymes page 67
1. star; 2. gold; 3. donkey; 4. angel; 5. manger

Rebus Fun page 67
1. Joseph; 2. infant; 3. stable; 4. census; 5. king

Scrambled Sentences page 70
1. The angel Gabriel appeared to Mary.
2. Mary visited her cousin Elisabeth.
3. Mary wrapped Jesus in swaddling clothes.
4. The shepherds found Jesus lying in a manger.
5. Herod sent soldiers to search for the child.

Unscrambling Activity page 76
1. hay; 2. tidings; 3. Joseph; 4. Gabriel; 5. Magi; 6. dream; 7. Caesar; 8. manger; 9. sheep; 10. Bethlehem; 11. Christ; 12. innkeeper; 13. Herod; 14. census

Underlining Activity page 76
1. born; 2. highest; 3. joy; 4. Lord; 5. womb; 6. God; 7. Jews

Unscramble a Verse page 77
"For unto you is born this day in the city of David a Saviour, which is Christ the Lord."

Vowel Activity page 79
Christ, Light of the World, Messiah, Good Shepherd, King of Kings, Lamb of God, Reedeemer, Saviour, Prince of Life, Prince of Peace, Alpha and Omega, Bright and Morning Star

Verse Voyage page 80
Blessed art thou among women and blessed is the fruit of thy womb.

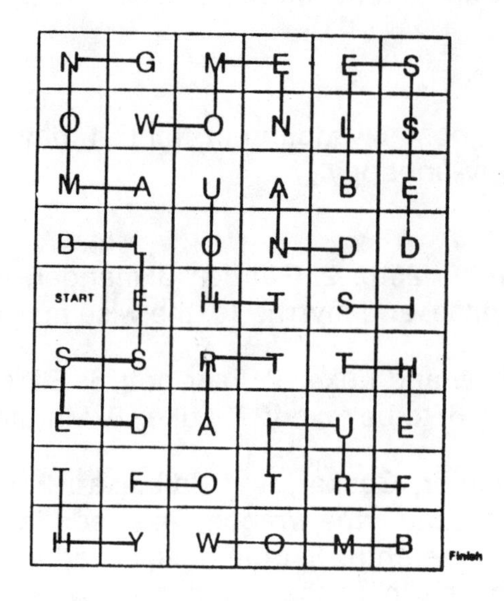

Word Search page 82

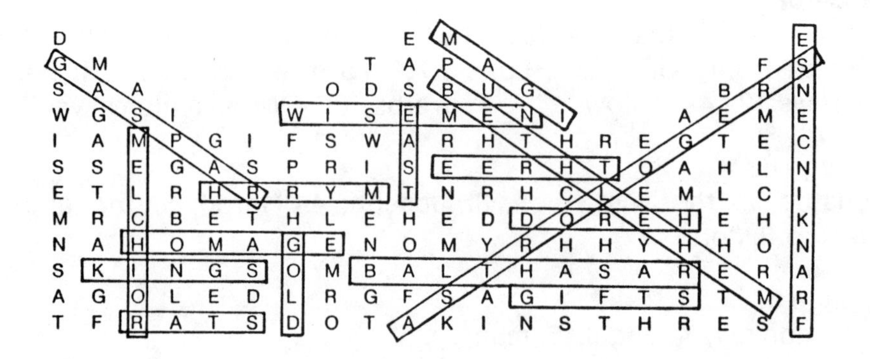

X Out Rhymes page 85
1. here; 2. shape; 3. stay; 4. stare; 5. far; 6. late; 7. comb; 8. anger; 9. fall; 10. called; 11. hail; 12. kind; 13. take; 14. nose; 15. barn; 16. chill; 17. God; 18. same

X Out Message page 85
". . . Fear not: for, behold, I bring you tidings of great joy, which shall be to all people."

Yuletide Messages page 88

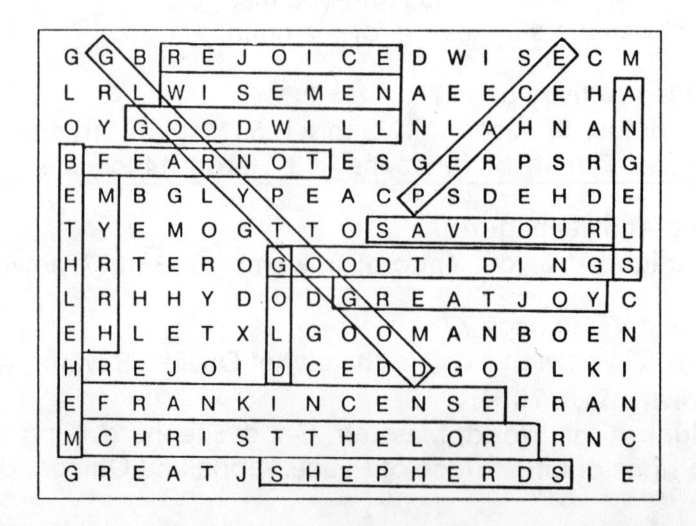